Imagine Childhood

imagine childhood

Exploring the World through Nature, Imagination, and Play

Sarah Olmsted

ROOST BOOKS

Boston & London

2012

Roost Books
An imprint of Shambhala Publications, Inc.
Horticultural Hall
300 Massachusetts Avenue
Boston, Massachusetts 02115
www.roostbooks.com

9 8 7 6 5 4 3 2 1

First Edition
Printed in China

♾ This edition is printed on acid-free paper that meets the
American National Standards Institute Z39.48 Standard.
♻ Shambhala makes every attempt to print on recycled paper.
For more information please visit www.shambhala.com.

Distributed in the United States by Random House, Inc.,
and in Canada by Random House of Canada Ltd

Designed by Lora Zorian

LIBRARY OF CONGRESS CATALOGING-IN-PUBLICATION DATA

Olmsted, Sarah.
Imagine childhood: exploring the world through nature,
imagination, and play / Sarah Olmsted.
p.   cm.
Includes bibliographical references.
ISBN 978-1-59030-970-4 (pbk.: alk. paper) 1. Games. 2. Play.
3. Imagination in children. 4. Creative ability in children. I. Title.
GV1203.O58 2012
790.1'922—dc23
2012000146

Contents

Acknowledgments

In gratitude . . .

Thank you to Shambhala Publications and Roost Books for your long-standing dedication to books with purpose and heart and for giving me the honor of sharing my voice here.

Thank you to Jennifer Urban-Brown for your insight, enthusiasm, and belief in this project. I couldn't have picked a better editor.

Thank you to Kiel Reijnen for being an on-call jack-of-all-trades. From executive chef to photo assistant to physics consultant, the images in this book owe a lot to your structural support.

Thank you to my dear friends whose beautiful children grace the pages of this book. Their youthful curiosity, intelligence, kindness, and humor are forever inspiring.

Thank you to my family, without whom none of this would be possible. From the words you shared here to the projects you helped create, it really does take a village. Each and every day you instill in me a belief in the unending beauty and potential of the world. This book is your book too.

And last but definitely not least, thank you, Trevor, for supporting my dreams, for keeping me well fed, and for giving me the space to wander in the woods of my imagination. You are my love, my life.

Preface

I'm not an astronaut. I'm not the secretary of education. I don't have eight PhDs. I'm not the mother of four grown children. I'm not an award-winning psychologist. I haven't been an educator for the past thirty years. What I am—in my best moments, when I see the world for all its potential and wonder—is a child. It is from that space that these pages come.

My path to writing this book can most easily be summed up as the outcome of a singular pursuit: chasing magic. The road hasn't been a linear one, but the goal has always been the same—to find places and activities where the unexpected can completely change the way I understand the world around me. In my early years I found this space in nature, in plants grown from seeds, in lightning, in the changing seasons, and in the flight of birds. As I grew older, I was enchanted by the magic of the classroom, by teachers who could expand and contract the universe like a pair of lungs, breathing life into the body of my imagination. My first real dream was to become a teacher so that I might perform this magic for someone else one day. Then, when I began to make my own way in the world, I followed that transformative space toward the arts and their capacity to challenge my assumptions, to ask me to examine every possible perspective, and to illuminate worlds I never even knew existed. This process of chasing magic led me to art school, to freelance design projects, and to the Field Museum of Natural History, where I developed interactive educational activities for permanent and traveling exhibitions. It was around this time, in the midst of this rich landscape of history and knowledge, that the seeds for the Imagine Childhood shop and blog were born.

When I was growing up, my mother had a toy store that saturated my early years with wonder. Each object was crafted with care, and often I would come to the shop after school and wander through its rooms. Many of the catalysts for my dreams and adventures came from that space. It wasn't just a toy store; it was an enchanted portal to everything I ever wanted to do or become. Years later, while developing activities for the museum, I felt that same sensation. The Imagine Childhood shop and blog were inspired by the spirit of both places.

So in 2008, after a year of development, my family and I launched imaginechildhood.com, a mixture of stories, activities, toys, and products that encourage exploration, creativity, and open-ended, unstructured play. Since its launch, I have continued to develop projects and activities for children and families on the blog. And now, through this book, I've begun a new leg of my journey . . . chasing the magic of childhood.

Into the Woods

Something about the place is familiar, but you can't quite put your finger on it. Off the bat, there aren't any landmarks or striking features that jog your memory to a specific time or event, but still, it feels like you've been there before. The way the trees move when the wind goes through them, the smell of damp earth, the deer trail stretching up the hill—they all point to something you can't quite reach.

With each step down the path, the colors get richer as the light becomes more and more filtered by the green canopy of aspen leaves above. Depending on the angle of the sun, white lupine flowers look like glowing candles flickering in and out, hiding behind swatches of grass only to reappear a moment later. Under your feet, leaves from seasons past crunch and crackle, and for just a moment, gravity feels different. As if somehow it's pulling a little less. As if the space between your feet and the ground has widened by the width of a single hair.

With this new sense of gravity, your steps are quicker, more playful than the daily gait you've become accustomed to. Their rhythm is a syncopated cousin to the pace you know, to the tempo you've settled into after decades of traveling from place to place. It's almost as if your feet have a mind of their own, a memory that your brain can't connect to. They lead you through the woods with a sense of purpose, a directive you can only hope to be clued in on at some point in the near future. Slowly but surely, your entire body moves into an uncanny naturalness. Your hands pick up sticks and throw them in the air so your eyes can see them float through the branches, weightless, if only for a millisecond. Your fingers pick blades of grass and weave them together. Your arms pull your body up the trunk of a tree. Your lungs breathe in the scent of leaves and sap.

More and more, you realize you have been here before. Glimpses of faded memories float by your eyes like passing clouds, changing their form with the wind. At first it's like an old movie, a story you learn as the scenes unfold. Then the characters slowly begin to come into focus—inch by inch, frame by frame. In the foreground, there's a small figure wearing a blue shirt and a pair of jeans. It's running and laughing, building forts from fallen branches, lying in the grass and gazing at clouds. Turning your head, you see the same shapes in the sky. Looking down, you see the same blue shirt. The faded memories have become focused on the world in front of you. On the grass where you're sitting. On the landscape of childhood.

The experience described above mirrors what I felt upon returning to the woods of my childhood, the very same woods that are pictured in the pages of this book. Walking into them, seeing the forts my siblings and I built decades ago, I felt a sense of place and potential that I hadn't in a long time. This return to the space of my early years brought back the mind-set of my childhood—the openness, the curiosity, and the endless possibilities. This book is structured around the same premise, one that asks you to travel back to your "woods," to look at the world from that perspective again, and to share in the adventure with your own children as they discover theirs.

The three main sections of this book focus on what I believe to be the keystones of childhood: Nature, Imagination, and Play. Within each category, you'll find essays and projects that dive into the richness of the subject. In the Nature section, you can learn how to make leaf capes and bird masks while thinking about the seasons, the magic of growth cycles, and the hidden potential in a pile of dirt. In the section on Imagination, you'll find instructions for making marionettes out of pinecones, boats from twigs and string, and tents for indoors and out. In the Play section, archery sets, do-it-yourself instruments, game bags, and cloth kites provide the backdrop for an exploration of what it means to live and learn through playful investigation. And finally, dotted throughout the entire book, you'll find recollections of childhood from my family and myself, a portrait of the lens through which we each saw the world in our own time and our own way.

Nature teaches us how the world works.
Imagination teaches us how to dream.
Play teaches us how to make our dreams real.

A Note on the Projects

Important Safety Notes: Some of the projects in this book are appropriate for children to make on their own; however, many require a collaborative effort between children and their caregivers. When projects call for the use of sharp scissors, saws, Exacto knives, hot glue, or Super Glue, these materials should be handled by adults or used under adult supervision. And finally, if using optical instruments to aid in your adventures (such as magnifying glasses, binoculars, telescopes, and so on) never use them to look directly at the sun.

As you go through this book, you'll find many different types of projects—some with detailed, step-by-step instructions and some that are more free-form and interpretive in structure. In either case, they are only meant to be stepping-off points, activities that might spark curiosity, an adventure, or an investigation. These projects are not about what is produced in the end (although that part is fun too); they are about the process of getting there. They're about the conversations that happen while making things together. They're about getting to know the world inch by inch. They're about exploring imaginary universes and running through real forests. They're about living in childhood, regardless of your actual age. They're about being a kid.

So, come on out and play . . .

PART ONE

Nature

*Looking, watching, listening, mimicking. Thousands of years
played out in the momentary interactions between leaves.*

Alone in the Wilderness is a 1966 documentary about a man who takes a few simple tools out to the woods and fashions a home and a way of life for himself.[1] The action isn't a revolutionary one; it's as old as time. Yet his slow and steady progress as he builds a home from felled trees, constructs a fridge from a moss-covered hole in the permafrost, and carves out a small garden seems nothing short of avant-garde. Each interaction is a riveting investigation into the limitless capabilities of the natural world, and the man's symbiotic relationship with nature is at once beautiful, inspiring, and romantic.

Romance is one of the most influential elements in culture and history, and nature is full of it. Nature is mysterious, exciting, full of adventure, and almost inexplicably alluring. It can inspire relationships that are far-reaching and long lasting; its wonders lure visitors across long distances; and its simple day-to-day functions (like sunrises and sunsets) can stop people in their tracks. It is for these reasons, among many others, that nature is so important to the lives of children (or anyone, for that matter). Nature teaches us how to fall in love with the world.

DISCOVERY

Few things are everything and nothing, but the natural world easily oscillates between both of these states. One moment, it's a textbook filled with page after page of science and history, and the next, it's an empty notebook waiting for new entries. Nature is a constantly changing chameleon. It can be precise and defined or open and nebulous. It's something that calls for definition by poets, artists, scientists, and writers, but it floats away before anyone can really nail it down. The only way to begin to grasp its shape is to jump right in.

It is easy to see how nature is everything, all you have to do is look out at a landscape. From the large components like trees and lakes and mountains, to small elements like anthills and microscopic pond scum, nature is undoubtedly full, every square inch is brimming with life, history, and intention. And it's not just horizontally so but also vertically, layer upon layer. Inside a forest you can see a fallen log with your eyes, inside that log you can discover the intricate world of insects with a magnifying glass, and you can even look all the way down to the cellular makeup of the wood with a high-powered microscope. There is always something new to find, to see.

For a child, having everything right there in front of you is an indispensable prospect. To be a kid is to ask questions . . . all day, every day. The intricacy of nature invites inquiry, and finding the answers to those questions only leads to further investigation. *Where does a bird live?* A nest. *What is a nest made of?* Grass and twigs and feathers. *Where do baby birds come from?* Eggs. *Where do birds keep their eggs?* In nests. Answers make insatiable appetites for knowledge, and nature is full of them, you just have to get to know her logic. You have to learn to be a good detective.

Like any activity, investigation requires a certain set of tools: observation, attention to detail, and an understanding of the relationships your subject has with other systems top the list. Nature provides the perfect playground to hone these skills. A simple walk through the woods can naturally prompt their use, but it helps to have a place to start. For children, having a common thread that connects the world of nature to their everyday experiences provides just what they need to get them going.

A good detective always starts with what they know best. What a child knows best is their immediate surroundings: their house, their family, their toys and objects, themselves. Using this vernacular they can make a bridge to the natural world. All of those things are there too. A bird has a nest (a house), a deer has a mother, a bear has eyes and ears, a wolf pup plays with friends. These types of similarities allow a child to feel like they belong, like they are part of the fabric of their environment. Once children feel like they are part of the environment, they feel even more comfortable asking questions and investigating. The world they see is now *their* world, full of new roads to travel and countless wonders to discover. Through its intricacy and openness, nature encourages a child to get to know the world they are moving through, to begin to understand how it all works.

THE STORY OF NATURE

Leaves move back and forth, brushing up against each other as the wind rushes through them, an action that has taken place for millennia in just the same fashion. One motion repeated across history. Nature is full of history; it's full of stories. Each tree ring tells the story of the year; each track tells the story of an animal's day; each leaf, the story of the season.

By investigating the natural world, children get to know their surroundings intimately. They find meadows that become their own secret kingdoms; they see birds and give them names; they make up tales about what may have happened in a particular hollow tree stump.[2] By personalizing the world around them, they become the authors of their environment.

Storytelling has always been a way to pass on important lessons and family or world history, as well as to make sense of things we may not yet understand. Finding the stories nature has to tell not only creates a greater connection to the natural world; it allows children to take part in a narrative that has been going on for a very long time. It allows them to make the story their own through time and discovery.

Perhaps the most important thing that comes with being the author of your own world is confidence. Without confidence, it's hard to make those necessary leaps into the unknown, to trust in your bearings and your ability to work with whatever situation may arise. When you know your world, you know the characters within it and can predict how they will interact in a given situation. You understand the setting and structure. Because of this, you can take risks, leaps in new directions, and if you fall, you know just how gravity works. By investing in the narratives of the natural world, children can feel the freedom to experiment within it.

AN EXTERNAL TOOLSHED: BUILDING A SENSE OF WONDER

To be a child is to look at the world in wonder. Even simple elements like rain and snow can be magical. And why shouldn't they be? They can transform the landscape almost completely in an instant (think snowstorms), make rainbows out of thin air, and produce brightly colored flowers from slimy brown dirt. If you think about it, nature *is* magic, but it's magic of the best kind: magic you can deconstruct.

The great thing about magic in general is that it takes all of our preconceived notions about how things work and challenges them, turns them upside down, and asks us to believe in a new world. The unfortunate thing about magic is that we often think it can be practiced only by very special individuals—magicians, elves, wizards, and the lot. Nature, on the other hand, is the people's magic. It performs many of the same fantastic "tricks" with none of the pretense. In fact, it even gives you a cheat sheet. Want to make a rainbow? Spray water into the air with a hose on a sunny day. Want to know where a butterfly comes from? Find a caterpillar or look for a cocoon. Want to see bright flowers magically appear? Plant a seed. Even the more complex wonders can be deconstructed and understood; they may need a bit more research and a few more tools, such as microscopes, but the answers are all there.

I spent a number of years developing interactive displays for a natural history museum, many of which were used to demystify natural wonders: tornadoes, earthquakes, genetics, the sound a long-extinct dinosaur would have made. Even as an adult, the ability to remake or approximate these phenomenal elements was nothing short of amazing. So much so that I felt like a kid every time I figured something out. I felt as though I had unlocked some hidden door to a new universe. Imagine feeling that every day, and you have childhood in a nutshell.

There is no greater skill than to learn how to make your own magic. It may not be easy, and it may take years of experimentation and failed attempts, but if you can make your own magic, you'll always have everything you need. Nature provides just the right tools for you to practice your craft.

AN INTERNAL WORKSHOP: EMBRACING SPACE FOR REFLECTION

Nature is everything. It's a classroom and a storybook, a lab and a playground, a magical universe. Yet perhaps one of its most underrated traits is its ability to be nothing—a blank canvas, formless—to disappear.

From the moment we wake up and get out of bed to the second we return there at the end of the day, we are inundated with images and information. One of the benefits of living in the time we do is the easy access to information. If you want to know what kind of bird is in a tree, look it up on your smartphone. If you want to see a rare puffer fish change colors, watch YouTube. These technological advances have made the world a smaller place in mostly wonderful ways. I've seen some pretty fantastic connections made between homeschooling groups that send each other nature specimens and identify each other's bug photos. The new generation of "pen pals" doesn't have to wait for letters to come in the mail; children can see each other on Skype. There is no doubt that technology has made the world of nature, and the world at large, more accessible. But in the pursuit of that access, with so many things to do and see, there is less and less space to just "be."

As much as kids need visual and intellectual stimuli, they need space to take everything in. We all do. The absorption of knowledge functions similarly to the ebb and flow of the ocean's tides. For stories, lessons, and details to come rushing back in when we need them, the tide has to go out. The waters need to recede and leave our shores quiet for a time.

If there is one thing that nature provides, it's space, and it produces it in spades. It is the perfect landscape to lose yourself in. To walk or run in. To lie down in and watch the clouds. To let your mind be still in. Hills don't have to be climbed; they can simply be looked at. Trees can lose their definition and turn into a dance of unfocused light and color. The stars can float overhead without purpose or intent. The world can be a quiet, calm place in which to dream.

Frederick Law Olmsted, the father of landscape architecture, once said that "landscape moves us in a manner more nearly analogous to the action of music than anything else."[3] Nature gives us music and space. All we have to do is find the beat and let the rest fall into place.

The projects that follow encourage you and your children to investigate and explore the magic of nature, from the changing seasons to the drama of birds and the power of dirt. Most important though, they ask you to open the door to the world around you, to jump right in and see what you may find.

1

Seasonal Magic

Growing up, there was always a distinct moment when I knew autumn had arrived. I'm not sure if it was the light, the temperature, or the sight of that first golden-tinged leaf on a tree, but as soon as I noticed it, everything changed. Summer always had a sort of length to it, not just in the hours of the day but in the slower speed of the activities and the way my mind would wander, moving at the pace of the shadows cast by the drifting sun. But from the moment fall hit, the energy was instantaneously different. The cooler air stirred faster movement from place to place, and the hours spent indoors at school heightened the intensity of the time spent outside. Suddenly each moment in the sun was a cherished one, as it stayed around just a bit less each day. Places I'd taken for granted during the preceding months were now special destinations. The space in autumn is closer somehow than in the other seasons, especially as the leaves begin to fall. Walking in the park, I'd take unnecessary detours just so I could wander through the patches of trees and enter those golden caves. I'd shuffle my feet along the ground to hear that familiar crunch and crackle, and everything else in the world would disappear. It was like the only thing that existed in the entire universe was that small bubble of golden trees and their shooting stars shaped like leaves. Growing up, autumn transformed my everyday world into the space of dreams. The season was magic.

Sometimes you can walk by a particular spot a million times before you realize there is something there. The day you do, you are forever changed, alert and receptive to what is around you. Seasons are like that for me. Growing up in a place like Colorado, with four distinct and dramatic times of year, I had the opportunity to get to know them all. Yet when I really think about it, that process didn't happen on its own. There were those magical, undeniable moments (like the one I just described) when the season took me on a journey—in the gold of autumn, in the quiet after a winter snowstorm, in the blooming branches of spring, and in the constellations of the summer sky—but my alertness to the tiny details came from another mechanism altogether. Whether it was a special winter hike, making a flower crown in the spring, walking to the swimming hole in the summer, or making jack-o'-lanterns in the fall, it was the activities that really focused the seasons for me, particularly those through which I learned something new. I remember the first time my mother pointed out a crocus and told me that spring would be here soon, because you only see that flower then. Little by little, as I learned more about the signs of the seasons, my relationship to them changed. Winter was no longer a monotonous string of cold, snowy months; instead, it became a diverse and varied landscape of small but distinct changes and events. There was always something new to watch for.

As an adult, every time I go for a walk, I catch myself looking a little more closely at the tree buds, listening for birdcalls, and watching for animal tracks on the trail. Getting to know the seasons as a child opened up the magic of the everyday—a magic that I might easily have walked by . . . a magic that deserves to be noticed.

SEASONAL CAPES

A single rectangular piece of cloth. Nothing special. There are countless copies of the same thing out there: rolled onto bolts in fabric stores; sewn into curtains, pillowcases, and clothes; covering bowls full of rising bread dough. They are decidedly commonplace. That is, until they become a cape. We all know what happens then.

Somewhere between the flip of fabric as it snaps through the air to land on a pair of shoulders and the tying of a simple knot to secure it, magic happens. I doubt that many scientists have studied the properties of handmade capes, but if they did, it would be a rich field indeed. Capes can make you invisible. They can loft you into the air at the slightest inclination. They can make time travel possible. Given these immense abilities, why would nature miss out on such a powerful object? It doesn't. Its capes just look like seasons.

Many of the magical and transformative capabilities found in a cape can also be prescribed to seasons. Once they blanket their wearer, everything changes. They can cause things to disappear and reappear. They can make something out of nothing. Seasons are the ultimate magic trick embedded in the fabric of our everyday experience.

Borrowing from their similar qualities in the realms of mystery and magic, Seasonal Capes not only make wonderful foils for make-believe and dress-up, but they also provide an opportunity to celebrate each and every one of the seasons . . . and all the activities and changes they bring. A spring cape covered in flowers can make the space to discuss the cycle of growth that happens during that time of year and to learn about all the flora and fauna that will be around. A summer cape can allow for conversations about warm-weather activities, plans for fort building, and new adventures. A fall cape can lead to autumn plans full of pumpkin pies, school, Halloween costumes, and colorful walks. A winter cape can spur discussions on hibernation, the crystalline structure of snow, the shortening days, and all the holiday celebrations.

Note: Although the shapes and decorations are all different, the construction of each cape is identical. Likewise, the materials list calls for enough fabric and ribbon for one cape, so if you're procuring supplies for all four capes at the same time, multiply the materials by four. The seasonal shapes can be modeled after any leaf, flower, or plant you like and cut to a size of 4"–6"; alternatively, you can use the templates in the back of this book.

- 1 yard lightweight muslin, 36"–44" wide
- Needle and thread or sewing machine
- Seasonal shape patterns (see pages 208–209)
- 150–160 seasonal shapes cut from scrap fabric (It seems like a lot, but you can often cut a stack of thin fabric pieces all at once, making five to ten shapes in the same time it takes to cut one.)
- 15–20 yards ribbon, ½"–¾" wide (I like cotton ribbon for this, but anything you have on hand will work.)

STEP ONE

Fold over the top cut edge of the muslin to the wrong side about ¼" and crease it by hand or with an iron. Take that folded edge and fold it down 1" more; sew along the bottom edge of the fold, making sure to leave a straight pocket the length of the top. This is where your ribbon drawstring will go through.

Since the two side edges are selvage edges, there is no need to finish them unless you prefer to (if you do, finish them before making the pocket for the drawstring). Fold the bottom edge over twice, ¼"–½" each time, and sew the edge down.

STEP TWO

Now that you have your cape base finished, it's time to start working on the embellishments. Collect or make your seasonal shapes: leaves, flowers, snowflakes, or any shape from nature you'd like to use. (See the "Suggested Activities" section that follows for ideas on selecting your shapes.) You may design your own or use the templates in the back of the book. You can also decorate the capes with just one shape or use a variety. If you make up your own, it can be helpful to cut them out of paper first and then use those templates to cut the fabric.

Cut fifteen to sixteen pieces of ribbon that are about 8" longer than the width of your muslin. Sew your seasonal shapes onto each ribbon about 3" apart (roughly ten shapes per ribbon), leaving about 4" of ribbon uncovered at each end. Using a sewing machine, sew back

and forth over the top of each shape to secure it completely (this only takes a couple of minutes per ribbon). If you are using many different fabrics, you may alternate colors and fabrics on each row. Or if you have just two or three different colors/textures, you might make one row of one color and another row of another color.

STEP THREE

Once you have all your shapes on the ribbons, you can put your cape together. Starting at the bottom of the cape, place the first ribbon so that the shapes hang slightly over the bottom edge and there is an equal amount of ribbon extending past either side. With a sewing machine (although this can also be done by hand), secure the ribbon in place by sewing through the center of the ribbon (right over the shapes again). Place the next ribbon on the cape in the same fashion (placing it so that the bottom edges of the shapes overlap the top of the previous row), and slide the ribbon slightly to one side so the shapes are offset from those on the first ribbon. This will give the cape a more natural flow and pattern. Repeat for each row, shifting the ribbons back and forth a bit to create a layered texture, until you reach the top of the cape. You can either leave a little space at the top, as with the capes shown here, or you can sew ribbons all the way to the top. Just make sure not to sew your drawstring pocket closed.

STEP FOUR

Once all the shapes are on the cape, you can either trim the excess ribbon on the sides of the cape to uniform lengths or fold the ends over and sew them down from the inside of the cape. Cut a piece of ribbon about 30" long for the drawstring (you can trim it once the cape is on). Attach a safety pin to the end of the ribbon and push it through the pocket at the top of the cape. Now your cape is done!

SUGGESTED ACTIVITIES

Cutting out the shapes for the various capes can take some time, which makes the perfect opportunity to discuss the season you are making the cape for. In this section, you will find a few suggestions for discussions to have during the crafting process and activities to do once the cape is made, but really, any seasonal activity you enjoy is great.

- Before starting work on a cape, it can be fun to make a trip to the library to look for books about the season in question. Pick up picture books, science books, audio books with seasonal themes (these can be great to listen to while cutting out shapes)—anything that will inspire conversations about the time of year.
- Talk about your favorite seasonal activities and pastimes. Make a list of the ones you want to do.
- Talk about what other cultures do to celebrate the different seasons.
- Talk about what the weather is like in other parts of the world at this time of year.
- Discuss what animals do during this time of the year.

Winter

- With your favorite winter books in hand, learn about how snow is formed and what types of crystalline structures make snowflakes.
- Go on a winter hike and look for shapes to include in your cape.

- Build a structure out of snow.
- Look for animal tracks in the snow and make up stories about where the animals were going and what you think they might have been doing.
- Sit quietly and listen to the sounds of winter.
- On really cold days, bring winter inside and write your own play. Use your cape as a costume for one of the players.

Spring

- Go on daily or weekly walks to the same locations so you can look for changes in the environment. Search for new leaves and flowers, listen for new birdcalls, and watch for animals and their tracks.
- Learn about the process a seed goes through to turn into a plant.
- Plan your garden and start seedlings indoors.
- Learn about the first plants to come out after winter and look for them on your walks.
- Make drawings of your favorite flowers.
- Fly kites in the spring breeze.

Summer

- Take hikes and learn about all the different trees you pass.
- Make leaf rubbings and turn them into nature study cards.
- Learn about summer constellations and look for them at night.
- Learn how different animals stay cool in the summer heat.
- Make paper fans and sail paper boats in ponds and rivers.
- Make up stories for your next campfire storytelling session.

Fall

- Learn why trees lose their leaves in the fall.
- Talk about harvesting crops and preserving food for the winter.
- Pick pumpkins and apples at a local farm.
- Make apple pies and apple butter.
- Carve pumpkins and make pumpkin pie and roasted pumpkin seeds.
- Write ghost stories for Halloween to tell around jack-o'-lanterns.
- Make fairy houses out of fallen leaves.

2

Out of the Dirt

A rabbit from a hat, a penny from behind your ear. Producing something from nothing has always been a job for a magician. . . . Or has it?

When I was a kid, my parents were always at work making something from nothing. Houses were transformed from shag carpet–covered chaos to sturdy, classic beauty. Dusty plots of dirt were turned into secret gardens, and string, felt, and pipe cleaners into fairies. All of this was accomplished not with a crew of seventy and a six-figure budget but with a couple pairs of hands and a few hours of free time at night and on the weekends. In their own way, my parents were alchemists. Watching them made me want to be one too.

Yet it wasn't until I performed an act of transformation myself that I really understood what that power meant. I could dive into the recycling bin for cardboard and paper, add a little tape, and come out on the other side with a shadow puppet theater. I could take something useless and make it useful. I could make useful things! From that moment on, I never stopped. Once I learned how to sew fabric, I wanted to learn how to use wood. Once I conquered woodworking, metal was next. After constructing objects for a while, I wanted to build a house. Now the list is even longer. Each time I gain a new skill, the process illuminates the opportunity of another, and my curiosity grows. Making things will do that to you.

Whether you're three or seventy-three, the act of assembling disparate materials into a new object is a profound one. In a world of ready-mades, it seems almost magical. Today, if you need a new chair, you go out and buy one. If you want a shirt, you take a trip to the mall. For many of us, life is filled with countless objects that have lost the connection to their source. We no longer have to "make" out of necessity, so sometimes we don't do it at all. But there's a hidden loss within the efficiency of our postindustrial times: process.

For children, process is everything. It's how they learn, how they absorb new lessons and activities. Working through projects, step by step, they begin to understand how the world they see came to be what it is today. Understanding process means knowing how to build the world you want to see. But in order to learn how to build the future, you have to start with the basics, and nothing is more basic than dirt.

Of all nature's materials, dirt is possibly one of the most underrated (except by those of you out there who are gardeners and know dirt, or rather soil, is king). It's a nuisance that's tracked into the house, making your floors dirty; it's the sand in your spinach that you couldn't wash out completely. It always ends up somewhere you don't want it. Yet for all its ability to be in the wrong place, when it's in the right place, there's no denying its versatility.

There are a million types of dirt and soil. From sandy dust that won't hold a shape to the clay used to make fine china. The only real difference between seeing dirt as a nuisance and dirt as an asset is knowing how to recognize its potential. And therein lies the beauty—dirt is supremely good at demonstrating the merits of looking for hidden potential.

Simple materials and hard work . . . process and patience . . . hidden potential. When you begin to unwrap the structures of the everyday—when you take a pile of dirt, add a little water, and build a house—you're taking your first steps toward the world of the future, toward becoming an innovator, an alchemist, and a magician.

EARTH HOUSE

Not unlike seeing a plant work its way through the earth for the first time, building structures from dirt can seem almost magical. Out from a pile of formless dust comes a sturdy structure, a place that could even become a home. It might take a little work and patience, but everything you need is right there beneath your feet. This project uses wooden forms and compacted mud to build a structure; the method is similar to one that has been used for thousands of years.

MATERIALS

- Wood or plywood, ¼"–½" thick, length and width based on the size of your house
- Waterproof wood sealer (Any water-based wood sealer from your local hardware store will do. They are often available in small containers as wells as spray cans, as with Poly-acrylic.)
- Scrap wood for door and window frames/spacers, screen frames, and dirt tamp
- Small piece of window screen, about 6"–10" square, or a mesh strainer (optional)
- Wooden dowel or square stock, ¼"–½" in diameter, length based on the height of your house
- Small screw or nail
- Painter's tape
- Bamboo garden stakes taller than your walls by at least 4"
- Dirt
- Water
- Vegetable oil or petroleum jelly
- String

On a piece of paper, draw the shape of the house or building you would like to make. Since the mud can take a few days to dry (more or less, depending on your climate), it's good to start with a small, four-sided structure so that you can see how everything works with the dirt composition and humidity. (The house pictured here is roughly 16" × 12" × 12".) After you know the shape and size of the building you want to make, measure out (or trace) the dimensions of the outside walls onto your wood or plywood.

STEP TWO

To make the inside panels for the form, you'll need to determine your wall thickness. The bigger your structure, the thicker the walls need to be. Given the dimensions of the house pictured (16" × 12" × 12"), we made the walls about 1½" thick; if they were any thinner, they would be too weak. If you would like to make something bigger, increase the wall thickness by about ½" for every additional 6" in height to provide the support you need.

Once you have decided on the thickness of the walls, measure in by that distance from either side of the outside walls on your original paper diagram; this shows you the size of the inside panels you need. (You don't need to measure in from the top and bottom of the outside panels; those measurements will remain the same for the inner panels.) Measure out (or trace) the dimensions of the inner panels onto your wood or plywood.

Note: Remember to take the thickness of the walls off either end rather than just subtracting the thickness of both walls from one side. This will ensure that you have the right shape to match your outside panels, which is important if you are working with a nonrectangular shape. If you are making simple rectangles, it won't matter either way.

STEP THREE

Cut out the outside walls and inner panels that you've marked on your wood. After you have all the pieces cut, seal the inside of the wood (the parts that will touch the dirt when you pack it in) with some sort of waterproof sealer and let it dry.

If you would like windows or doors, you can make the spaces for them by cutting blocks of wood that are the same thickness as the walls to the desired height and width and inserting them between the inner and outer frames. If you are making windows, simply fill your wall up with mud to the level that you would like to be the bottom of your window opening and then drop the spacer block in.

STEP FOUR

Besides the frames for the walls, two other tools are important for making mud structures like this: a screen for sifting the dirt and a tamp for compressing the mud. For the screen, you can either use a wire mesh strainer from your kitchen, or you can make a sifting screen by constructing two identical wooden frames (about 6"–10" square). Sandwich a piece of screen between them, making sure the sharp edges don't stick out beyond the frame. Then glue, screw, or nail the two frames together.

To make the tamp, simply cut a square piece of wood that is the same width as your walls (inside the frames) and screw or nail this to the end of a dowel or square piece of wood that is longer than the height of your tallest wall by a few inches.

STEP FIVE

When you have picked out the location for your building and are ready to set up the structure, I've found that a little painter's tape goes a long way toward helping to set up the frames. Trying to set up without it can lead to a lot of frustration, because the walls like to fall down just when they are almost all in place. A few strips of tape on the corners will hold the interior and exterior frames together so you can position them easily. When the forms are where you want them, drive the bamboo garden stakes into the ground inside the inner panels and outside the outer panels (not in the space in between them, since that is where the mud will go).

STEP SIX

Here comes the really fun part: the mud. The best dirt composition contains a relatively high level of clay, but for the most part, whatever you have in your backyard should work. If you're worried about structural integrity, you may add a bit of straw or grass to your mixture. Using your screen, sift out any big rocks or stones that are in the dirt. This makes for a fairly consistent texture that will be more structurally stable. Since the

mud will be compressed, it's better to have an excess of dirt so you don't run out midprocess. For the house shown here, I used about a five-gallon bucket's worth. Add water a little at a time, mixing with your hands, until the dirt is wet enough to form a ball but not slimy or sloppy—sort of like a modeling clay texture.

STEP SEVEN

With the mud ready and your forms in place, it's time to start making the walls. To do this, put a little oil or petroleum jelly on the inside of the forms so the mud won't stick to them. Roll the mud between your hands and drop pieces of it between the frames; when you have about an inch of mud all along the bottom of the frame, use the tamp to compact it, making an even layer by stamping it up and down. Repeat this until the form is completely filled with compacted earth. If you notice your form starting to open up at the corners once you put some mud in, simply wrap a little string around the outside of the frame and tie it tight.

Now it's time to wait. Once the top edges are dry (this could take a few days), carefully remove the stakes and the outer frame. If the frame sticks at all, loosen it with a spackle knife or something similar; slide it between the mud and the frame, then apply a little pressure and wiggle it back and forth. Once the outside frame is off, remove the inside frame in the same manner and allow the structure to dry the rest of the way without the forms.

STEP NINE

If you wanted windows and doors, remove the spacers carefully once the structure is mostly dry. You will need to reinforce these openings with frames made from scrap wood. Remember that the top piece (the lintel) should always go on top of the two side pieces, which in turn support the structure. Make frames for all the windows and doors. If you would like a roof, you can make one out of sticks and straw or a little wood, depending on your preference. (I prefer to have no roof so that play can also happen from the top of the house, but the structure falls apart faster without one.)

STEP TEN

Now that you know how to make some-thing from nothing, keep designing! Make plans for cities and villages, build minimuseums—the possibilities are endless.

In the Earth

Growing up in Colorado, I remember being fascinated with the surface of the earth and what lies beneath it. In observing all that burrowed beneath and sprung up above, the earth seemed to be an infinitely variable palette of raw and vital materials. I remember watching my mom water the garden in the backyard. At first, the soil appeared dry and rough from the heat of the summer sun. With a hose and a careful hand, my mom would intuitively spray just the right amount of water onto the different flowers and vegetables. She would saturate the earth just enough to prevent flooding and keep from destabilizing the soil and all the plants that made their home in it. When I looked closely, I could see the earth literally drink up the water. Initially, it would pool up on the surface and then get mysteriously pulled down into the dirt. While this was happening, the texture and color of the soil would change dramatically from pale and dry to soft and dark. In the end, both the plants above and the earth below looked healthy and happy.

Dirt, plants, rocks, and water—the character of our environment is defined by the balance and interaction of these simple yet complex substances and compounds. I knew this, or at least felt it, growing up. Perhaps inspired by years of watching my mom water her garden, I remember making a mud pit in the backyard. Earth that was once solid became completely fluid and viscous. I started by digging a large hole near the jungle gym, not far from the garden. The hole was large enough to sit in. When I sat in the bottom of it, my head was just above the level of the nearby lawn. Looking at the walls of dirt surrounding me, I could see rocks, roots of plants, worms, and bugs in the interwoven layers of earth. I remember filling the hole with water and then adding the dirt I had displaced from digging back into the hole, mixing it into the water with my feet, legs, arms, and hands. I could create different kinds of mud by adding more or less dirt and water. Where once I had stood on the solid surface of the earth, now I was partially submerged within and coated with it. Looking back, I think more than wanting to have fun and make a mess in the backyard, I wanted to better understand how plants, water, rocks, and earth combined to create the world we live in.

Digging into the dirt when I was young and discovering everything it held continued to help me make sense of what was really happening both beneath and above the surface as I grew older. Walking down the street, I could see bits of sand and pebbles and rock cast into the solid sidewalks and asphalt roads that led me to adventures in my neighborhood. I remember the first time I saw the sidewalks being replaced with new concrete. Fluid concrete, not unlike the mud in my backyard, was placed and then smoothed flat. At first, it looked dark gray and wet, but later, over time, it became pale gray and rock solid. Concrete, I was told, was similar to mud but composed of a different and unique blend of natural ingredients that made it transform from a fluid material into a durable and solid surface. The streets and sidewalks were themselves man-made geologic features, not unlike my backyard experiments. Even though the sidewalks and streets were more durable than my grass and dirt structures, I remember seeing them erode and wear out from weather and use. I noticed cracks and lifts in the surface of the sidewalk caused by tree roots growing underneath. Weeds and plants would grow up through cracks in the pavement.

Traveling with my family expanded my mysterious mix of knowledge and fascination with earthly materials. I remember finding a large chunk of volcanic; glassy smooth obsidian at a rock shop in Montana. I was told it had once been fluid, dangerously hot lava. It had solidified and broken off into a jagged and smooth glassy shard that was shaped like the face and head of a lion. Was lava like the mud in my backyard? Could molten earth flow like rivers did?

On other family trips, I remember the many times that I was led to a mysterious and magical place along a river, where moss and flowers grew on the side of a cliff and natural springwater flowed down into the swimming hole at its base. There, surrounded by the magic of earth and water, I gleaned the mythology and history of my family. Rocks, dirt, plants, and water merged into one interwoven fabric of beauty and memories over time. I still return to this location as an adult and reconnect with my early thoughts, discoveries, and experiences in nature.

—Jared

3

First Impressions

Green, slimy, and often smelly, pond scum isn't exactly the first thing that comes to mind when you think of beauty. It lives more in the realm of, let's say, *ick*. It obscures clear, crisp waters and makes swimming in them a less-than-pleasurable experience. But put it under a microscope, and it's gorgeous. Suddenly, you see beautiful, opalescent, microscopic creatures moving about their daily chores unaware of our distaste for their architecture. Pond scum is a lesson in first impressions.

As a child, there is so much to take in. Everything is big and bright and new. Just processing the surface of all that you might encounter in a day can be more than enough. So the prospect of taking the time to see beyond that top layer can sometimes be daunting. Yet that's often where the good stuff is. The crystal inside the geode, the butterfly inside the cocoon—all that's required to see them is a little patience and attention.

Patience, though, is a learned behavior. Few of us possess that grace straight from the womb. We have to find it, cultivate it, and nurture it. Many activities can bring about this transformation, but in all instances, they have some sort of magnificent reward. Bird-watching is a perfect example.

Many animals have dramatic components to their physiology. There are lizards and fish that change color at whim. There are baboons with bright purple flashes amid their brown fur. And then there are the birds. Oh, those birds. Simple, demure, and slight one moment; fantastic, dramatic, and larger than life the next. They can slip by unnoticed, or they can turn around and stop traffic. Yet you have to catch them at just the right moment; otherwise, they'll fly by as a gray, unassuming version of themselves, and you'll be none the wiser.

Bird-watching is all about patience. If you set out wishing to see your favorite species within the first ten minutes, you will be sadly disappointed. Birding is as much about observing the quiet and stillness of the woods as it is about seeing that beautiful flash of colorful feathers against the green canopy. Birds don't appear on our schedule; they show up on theirs. They ask us to wait and watch, to believe in the potential of the unexpected, to seek hidden treasure in an ordinary field. Luckily, children are always on the lookout for hidden treasure.

In the same sense that everything is new to a child, everything also has infinite potential. Trees can come from seeds or crystals. Clouds can be filled with rain or rainbows. As we grow and define more and more of the world, such potential becomes limited by our observations and experiences. Engaging in activities that promote a belief in the unexpected, that ask us to look beneath the surface and beyond first impressions, helps us think of potential as it should be—open-ended and unlimited.

BIRD OF PARADISE MASK

Anyone who has ever played peek-a-boo with a baby knows that most kids love surprises. Just like those beautiful birds that unexpectedly swoop right by your head, a surprise from nowhere can instantaneously change your world. Having your own surprise to let out anytime you wish means you can change the world for someone else, and that is exactly what this great mask does. Brown and simple on first inspection, the mask allows its wearer to go unsuspected until he or she decides to make a big impression and, in an instant, become a beautiful, colorful bird.

- Mask pattern (see page 211)
- 4 squares wool felt, 12" × 12" each
  (2 brown or gray squares, plus 1 each
  of two different colors)
- 1 square cotton muslin, 12" × 12" (for
  the lining)
- 1 yard ribbon, 1" wide
- Needle and thread

STEP ONE

Using the template, cut two mask pieces
from your brown or gray felt and one
from the muslin. Depending on your

child's age, the eyeholes may need to
be closer together or farther apart. I
suggest cutting the pattern out of paper
first and testing it. That way you can
move the eyeholes together or apart to
best fit your child. You can also change
the overall shape of the mask or the
feathers to more closely match the birds
of your choice.

Stack the three pieces together
with the muslin on the bottom. Cut
two 18" long pieces of ribbon for the
ties and place each ribbon between
the two sheets of felt on either side of
the mask. Secure with pins. You may

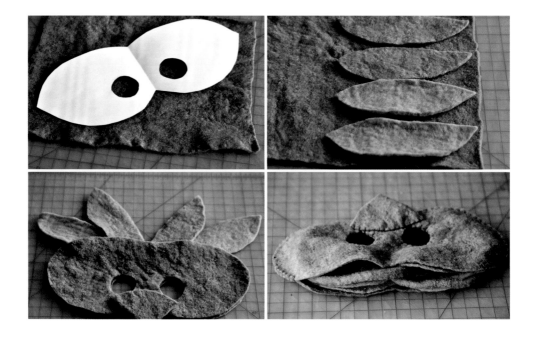

also wait to position the ties until after the mask is complete. If you choose this method, you can simply sew them on from the back side of the mask.

Once you have the ties in place, hand sew the mask together using a blanket stitch (see photo below) along the bottom, the sides, and 1½" of the top on either side (measure from the top of the ribbons) leaving the center section of the top open. Separate the two felt pieces and finish stitching the mask along the top edge by sewing together only the muslin and the felt piece di-rectly on top of it. The front top piece of felt should remain unattached to leave an open pocket along the top of the mask.

STEP TWO

Using the same blanket stitch, sew around the insides of the eyeholes, sewing through all three layers. Cut the triangular nose piece (from the template) out of felt and center it between the eyes just below the eye-holes. Attach it to the mask along the top edge only, with the point facing downward.

STEP THREE

Cut two 1" × 12" pieces of the brown or gray felt and roll them up into 12" long antennae. Sew the roll closed using a blanket stitch; make sure to give an extra tug at the end of each stitch, as this helps to make them roll and curl just a little when they're done.

Cut four feather pieces out of the colored felt using the template (two each of the two different colors). Then, pinch a small section close to the bottom and stitch the pinch in place. This puts a bit of a cone shape into the feathers and gives them more structure and strength.

STEP FOUR

Taking the four colorful feathers, layer them on top of one another with the pinched sections in the center and two feathers sticking out to either side (you will be able to fan them out later after they are sewn). You can either put two of the same color in the first two layers or alternate colors. One of each color should be pointing in each direction if you would like your mask to look like the one pictured.

Once you have the stack, sew several stitches through all of the layers, back and forth until they feel quite secure.

Once those are in place, lay the two antennae on top of the stack in the center and stitch them down as well.

STEP FIVE

Through the opening on the top of the mask, put in the stack of feathers and antennae, centered just above and between the eyeholes. Attach it to the mask with a few stitches through the back two layers just in the center of the stack. Once this is complete, tack it to the front of the mask from the inside, being careful not to go all the way through the felt. This way you won't be able to see the stitches on the face of the mask. Once this is done, hide the pieces inside the mask, between the layers of felt, and when it's time . . . pull them out as a big surprise!

SUGGESTED ACTIVITIES
Before

Since the mask is based on tropical birds of paradise, this project can be a good excuse to learn more about these wonderful creatures. A trip to the library or the zoo before starting could also be a great way to get some inspiration for colors and shapes. You could draw pictures of birds from books, take photos of them at the zoo, and learn about their colorful attire. In short, take the time to really get to know your subject and have fun with the process. So often the focus is on the end result rather than the steps it takes to get there. What I've found, though, is that the more time and care you take along the way, the more the end result is truly appreciated.

During

Since some of the construction will require the help of experienced hands, younger helpers can take the time that they aren't crafting to write or make up stories about the character/bird they will be when they put on the mask. Where will they go? What will they do? Who will they meet? Is the mask magical? Perhaps its wearer will look so much like a bird that the elves and fairies won't hide from them when they walk through the woods. Does the mask give the person who wears it the ability to fly? Collect these stories/drawings in a notebook or a folder to refer to later when you're looking for dramatic play ideas.

After

Once the mask is complete, take it, along with the stories and plays that were written during the craft time as well as any bird-watching supplies you might have (a set of binoculars, bird guides, and so on), to your favorite cluster of trees. When you get there, make a fort out of sticks or blankets to use for play or to function as a bird blind. You could play hide-and-seek, eye spy, tag, or most important, just enjoy the quiet of the woods. Who knows, maybe you'll see a beautiful bird.

4

Building from Nature

Down a small deer path about five hundred feet, there was a grouping of a few aspen trees with an outcrop of medium-sized boulders in the center. It was beautiful but by no means the most picturesque spot around. What it did have was the illusion of privacy, of a space that was all my own. No matter that my mother could easily see me from where she sat. I couldn't see her, so for all intents and purposes, I was alone, free to explore my secret world and all the adventures that came with it.

Every summer for many years, I spent hours and hours there. In my head, I spent lifetimes: one life as a magician who could perform any type of magic imaginable, one as a girl rescued by elves and transported to their kingdom, one as an explorer finding new lands. The list went on and on. Each day, there in the woods, was full of epic adventure, yet I never spent a single minute preparing for those adventures. I never packed a bag full of tools and materials—I didn't have to. Everything I could ever dream up was already there. If I needed a sword, I would find a good stick. If I needed a crown, I would weave together aspen leaves. My little grove could supply me with anything I desired.

Materials in nature have a way of understanding efficiency to the highest degree. The same basic building blocks are used for many elements, and complex structures are often just millions of repetitions of simple structures. Nature is full of fractals.

Flowers and trees are perfect examples of fractal beauty. Dramatic and majestic, they seem utterly unique and impossible to replicate. That is, until you break them apart. On a component level, they're just a grouping of repeated shapes. A rose is the same petal arranged over and over again in a spiral pattern. A tree is a system of branches based off of a simple repeated configuration. Beginning with the basic Y created by the trunk and the bottom limbs, small branches follow the pattern of large branches, and so on.

Seeing the world through fractals—the simple parts that make up the complicated whole—is a powerful thing. Anyone who has ever attempted to complete a large project knows this fact well. If you want to run a marathon, you can't just walk out the door and do it with no prior training. What you can do is begin to build up your stamina; you can start with one step and then add another. Soon addition will add up to completion, and you'll be at the end of your race.

When you're a kid, everything is a big project because everything is new. You don't know where to start since you haven't been there before. Knowing how to look at the whole and break it apart into smaller pieces solves this problem. It gives you a place to begin. Nature and its fractals teach us to do this. They teach us how to solve problems and how to make anything we can dream up.

MAPLE LEAF HOUSE

Even some of the most strikingly beautiful elements in nature can be replicated easily by a child's hands. Building a Maple Leaf House combines the ingenuity and magic of being a kid in the woods, improvising your own tools and methods, with the production of something simple, beautiful, and useful. This house becomes a microcosm of an imaginary world where you can play for hours and hours, with a new plot and a new adventure every day.

- Leaf pattern (see page 210)
- 8 squares wool felt, 12" × 12" each (various leaf colors)
- Needle and thread
- Sticks and branches

STEP ONE

Using the pattern, cut out eight leaf shapes from the felt. You can reduce or enlarge the pattern, depending on how large or small you would like your house to be.

STEP TWO

Once you have your pieces cut, take two of the leaves of the same color and sandwich them together. Using a blanket stitch, sew them together along the sides and top, leaving the bottom edge of the leaf open. Repeat this three more times so that you have four double-sided leaves.

STEP THREE

Lay out three leaves with one on the bottom and the other two layered on top and rotated to either side just a bit.

Tack the bottom leaf and the left top leaf together at the first indentation of both leaves just before the center section of each leaf, as shown in the photo. Do the same for the right top leaf.

Align the open end of the fourth leaf to the open end of the bottommost leaf in your stack. Slide the fourth leaf under the bottom leaf and position them so that the first indents on the left and right sides of the openings align, as shown in the photo. Tack the leaves together at each of these indents. Now fold the three top leaves up like a hinge and form the leaf house into a shape you like. Tack the top leaves to the bottom leaf where needed to maintain the shape. You may also add a few more tacks to the upper leaves to add more strength, and even a few more leaves if you'd like to make a larger structure (although only four are needed to make the basic form).

The house is now essentially done. It is a soft house that can be squished down into a bag and then popped up again. If you would like more structure, on your next trip out to the wild, collect a few small sticks and break them to the length of the leaf. Insert them into the open bottom end of each leaf and up to the top point; your construction will instantly become a sturdy little fairy house.

NATURE FAIRY

A pretty little house should be inhabited by an equally pretty little fairy. When I was growing up, my mother made versions of the ones you see here for my siblings and me in almost every variation, from rose and mushroom fairies to maple leaf sprites, many of which are still around today. Although a little more "loved" than they once were, these fairies from my childhood are still beautiful and, above all, pretty magical. The following instructions help you to make the basic body and head for your own fairy or sprite—a blank canvas for a million different little magical creatures to make their way into the world.

MATERIALS

- - - - - - -

- 1 pipe cleaner
- About 3 yards of medium- to light-weight yarn
- Needle and thread
- 1 square knit fabric, about 2" × 2"
- Felt or cloth scraps and wool roving for clothes and hair, embroidery thread for eyes and mouth
- About a 1" ball of wool

STEP ONE

Cut the pipe cleaner in half, then fold each piece in half. Twist one of the folded pipe cleaners together about ¾" down from the bend; this makes the head. Take the second folded pipe cleaner and place it under the twist (the neck) in the first, then cross the right side over to the left and vice versa to make the arms. Cut ¼" off the end of each arm.

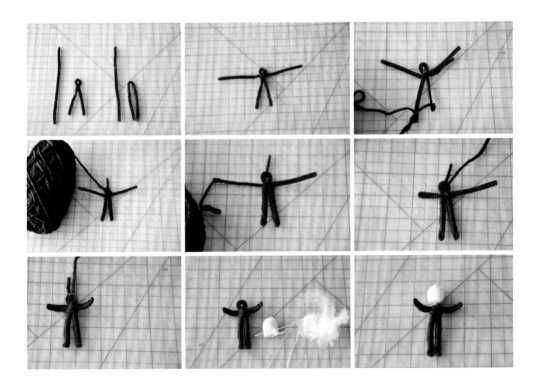

Now you need to wrap the body with yarn. Place one end of the yarn at the back of the neck and wind it first around the body and then down one leg. At the bottom of the leg, fold the pipe cleaner up onto itself ¼" and wrap it tightly with yarn around the leg. When this is secure, wrap your way back up to the body. Run the yarn down the leg again (do not wrap it this time because that would make the leg too thick; just go straight down); wrap some yarn around the ankle a couple of times, then wind it back up the leg. Repeat for the other leg, all without cutting the yarn.

When the legs are done, wrap one arm to the end of the wire; fold the arm in half. Wrap the yarn once around the body and out to the end of the arm again, leaving ⅛" unwrapped near the end so you have a tiny loop for the hand. Wrap back toward the body. Cross over the body and repeat the process for the second arm.

Once both arms are done, wrap the yarn over one shoulder and across the midsection, crossing from left to right and then right to left so you have an X shape. Cut the yarn about 6" away from the body. Using a large needle, sew a

stitch knot and run the thread through the body to the other side, cutting off any leftover string.

Cut the knit fabric into a small rectangle, about 1" × 1½". Fold it in half, with the two short edges aligned together. Hand sew the top edge of the tube you've made (the shorter side) with a running stitch; gather the fabric and tie it off, but don't cut the thread. Now sew down the side with a regular stitch and tie it off, but leave the thread and needle attached. Turn your tube inside out and stuff it with a little bit of wool. Sew a running stitch around the open end of the head, then place it over the pipe cleaner loop on the body. Pull the thread to gather the fabric, and the head of your fairy will magically appear. Make a knot to secure it, then run the thread back and forth through the neck to fasten it to the body. Once it's secure, wrap the thread around the neck a few times before running it down through the body and cutting it off.

Now that you have your completed fairy body, it's time to add the face, hair, and clothes. If you would like to add eyes and a mouth (some prefer to leave the face without them), simply run a needle and thread (with a knot at the end) through the back of the head to the outer point of one of the eyes. Make a small stitch and come out at the inner corner of the other eye; make another small stitch that exits the back of the head. Give the thread a little tug to make a bit of an indent at the eyes and tie it off. Repeat the same process for the mouth but use only one slightly longer stitch.

For the hair, you can sew wool roving on top of the head and cut it to your favorite style, or you can use thread. Alternatively, you can simply make a cap and forego the hair all together.

For the clothes, follow your preferences for items in nature that you love the most. When you look closely, seemingly complicated blossoms are often actually just layers of simple shapes that can easily be cut out of felt and made into a beautiful skirt or tunic. The clothing of the fairies pictured here was constructed by layering "skirts" (strips of felt with a running stitch through the top to make the waist) that had petal and pine shapes cut into them. To make a leaf tunic, simply cut out two identical leaf shapes, place them on the front and back of your fairy, and tack them together over either shoulder and at either side of the waist.

STEP FIVE

Empty houses of any kind need a few amenities, a few comfortable places to rest weary bones and nourish growing families. A fairy house is no different. Fairies, elves, and gnomes need a comfortable couch after a long day's work just as much as the rest of us. Since the forest has so many wonderful materials at hand, have fun improvising these furnishings. I especially love it when there is a rope swing and a tiny tree house nearby.

Ice Storm

As a child, I was always gazing off into the distance, registering the shapes I could find in the faraway landscape. The shape of the shore encircling a lake, the road as it enveloped the hills leading down to the water. The trees filtering light around the soft waves. I wasn't interested in anything close-up; I loved sights at a distance.

One morning, I awoke to glistening. Everything sparkled. Not just the lake—the road appeared dusted with diamonds, houses shimmered, and the trees glistened, as did everything in between and beneath. The sun was shining, and the temperature was freezing. An ice storm had struck during the night. Everywhere my eyes landed, surfaces were caked in ice twinkling with a rainbow of colors.

To my joy as I stepped from the house, I felt as if I were venturing out into wonder. Gazing upward, I was met with a canopy of interlocking branches all tied together by glittering ice, the sun streaming through. Below, rocks that had been gray were now rich, textural browns. The thickets and gardens shone in a new light, revealing pathways I hadn't noticed before. There were tunnels created by our collies, Monty and Rocky, leading off in new directions.

Had I just stepped out of my warm, cozy home and into another world? My imagination was now awake, wandering, dancing in the flashes of light, disrupted only by the cracking of the ice. This world was fragile, breaking easily under my feet and from my touch. It was a magical world where color and light played, creating shadows that only I could name. Mysterious sounds could be heard; the trees groaned under the weight of the ice. Crackling and popping could be heard around corners just out of sight, the sun created the music of melting.

By the time I returned home, drops of water were splashing all around as the sun did its job of warming the earth. I was cold, but my imagination was fed with a rich food of images, sounds, and textures that—I'm delighted to say—have lasted a lifetime.

A year or two later, I discovered that I was extremely farsighted and needed glasses with bifocals, but that day's ice storm and my lack of full sight brought me a gift that I truly needed to set my imagination to flight.

—Deb

5

Inside Outlines

In one of my early art classes, we had to make contour drawings, which is essentially drawing the outlines of things. Try as I might, I was never able to get it right. Somewhere in the middle of that long line I'd lose my way. I'd double back, retrace my steps, and still end up going in circles, my quest for form lost in the tangles of my pen. This wasn't the case for my older brother. From an early age, he was drawing portraits, comic strips, and the like with ease and fluidity. Perfect outlines and gestures that could tell you exactly what was going on. If you looked at his drawings, you were there, seeing what he wanted you to see, reading the image he created with no need for translation. To this day, when I make a line drawing, it still needs subtitles.

As a kid, I blamed my lack of proficiency in illustration on my unskilled hand. Why, oh why, couldn't I get it to move the way I wanted it to? I tried drawing fast to see if that helped. Nothing. I tried drawing slow. Nope, that didn't work either. Just when I was about to give up, I learned that it wasn't my hand, my skill, or the speed. It was my eyes.

That's not to say my vision is poor. In fact, I've never had to wear glasses in my life. But that doesn't mean I was looking or that I was really seeing. In my effort to follow the outlines perfectly, I was missing all the material in the middle—the colors and shapes, the building blocks of form.

Everything is made up of colors and shapes. A stop sign is red and octagonal. Mountains are composed of different triangular forms. People have squares and circles and trapezoids of different colors in their faces. Start with one, slowly add the rest, and you'll end up with a perfect likeness. Once you can see the shapes, you can make anything.

Changing your perspective can make a world of difference. I am a firm believer in the idea that anyone can do anything. We may not all be able to do it the same way, and some of us may have more facility in a particular area than others, but we can all do everything given the right methodology. Taking the time to look at a problem from every angle, to practice trying on different perspectives, means one thing: you are that much closer to doing everything you ever dreamed of.

COLOR AND SHAPE ACTIVITIES

Seeing is such a natural process that we don't often think about what goes into understanding an image. How the eyes work to focus light and deliver a signal to the brain, a signal that then needs to be deciphered for meaning. On paper, it all seems infinitely complex, yet we do it every second of every day.

Really seeing what you are looking at, though, is a slightly different process. It's more about making connections than sorting data. It's about understanding what's not there as much as about seeing what is. It is a conscious act versus a passive activity. Making drawings as a kid, I had to learn how to see what I was looking at in order to interpret it into something I could use to share my thoughts and ideas—to sift through all of that information and come out the other side with a story.

Shapes are one of the first things we get to know in the world when we make our way into it. We investigate them with our fingers and follow them with our eyes. Even if we don't yet know their names, we can separate and stack similar shapes from a very early age.

Images, whether bucolic landscapes or urban settings, are all made up of the same shapes. A forest might have more circles and triangles than a city street corner, but they can each be composed of the same elements. The point of making shape drawings and playing shape games is to understand how all of these parts and pieces go together. To look at an environment and search for all the squares, then look again for all the ovals. To understand the relationship between a bee's honeycomb and a New York City skyscraper.

Since color is one of the easiest signifiers, making drawings based solely on one hue can be a great filter as well. Like the plates of a lithograph, color drawings separate an image into layers that make no distinction between leaves and grass, glass and water. Materials mix more fluidly, while colors have more distinct boundaries. Inside the color wheel, a polar bear and a daisy live in the same house.

Visual stories are everywhere, and sometimes all it takes to see their thread is a little shift in perspective. A simple filter to separate the big stones from the small ones, to organize a jumble of parts and pieces into a working engine. Making shape drawings and color drawings can be a great way to start this process.

SHAPE DRAWINGS

The process for making shape drawings is really simple. Essentially, you just choose a color for a particular shape (for example, green for all the square shapes), then look at the landscape in front of you and draw only those shapes using the color you've chosen, making sure to keep them in the same orientation they are in, in real life. After that, pick another color and a different shape and start a new drawing. Repeat as many times as you like. What do the different drawings look like? What patterns do they make?

COLOR DRAWINGS

The process for making color drawings is the same as that for shape drawings except that color is not an arbitrary choice, since you can draw with the same color you're seeing. The interesting thing that can happen when making these monochromatic drawings is that you may begin to notice the real colors that make up the images and objects in front of you. You may think the sidewalk is just gray, but when you squint your eyes and look at only the colors, you might see that it is actually blue and green in some places or that it isn't gray at all but really a light shade of purple.

COLOR AND SHAPE GAMES

Playing games with color and shape can be a great way to practice really seeing what you are looking at. Awarding different point values to different hues makes children much more inclined to search over an entire scene for a tiny speck of blue. Likewise, if finding triangles is the goal, kids may notice that both mountains and pine trees are triangular in shape or that a One Way street sign is a rectangle and a triangle put together. If you're interested in having a scavenger hunt/race, rather than collecting points, players might have to go to a location, find a blue triangle, and take a picture of it. Or they may need to find something yellow to collect from a different spot before moving on.

COLOR AND SHAPE MAD LIBS

Use random colors and shapes to help tell stories. A combination of eye spy and mad libs, this game assigns random emotions to colors and actions to shapes. Before the game starts, players can make up the guidelines for that particular game. They might look like this:

COLOR EMOTIONS:
  Yellow = Happy
  Green = Excited
  Blue = Sad
  Red = Worried

SHAPE ACTIONS:
  Square = Running
  Triangle = Sitting
  Circle = Walking
  Rectangle = Skipping

As the storyteller begins a story, the other players look around and announce the colors and shapes they see when they would like to change the direction of the story. If a child shouts out, "Yellow," then the storyteller has to make up something happy. Likewise, if another player shouts, "Square," the characters in the story have to start running. The meanings of the colors and shapes can change completely between games.

COLOR COOKING

How can you cook a rainbow? Work your way through the color wheel with things like strawberry shortcake, carrot soup, lemon sorbet, marinated kale, blueberry crumble, and purple

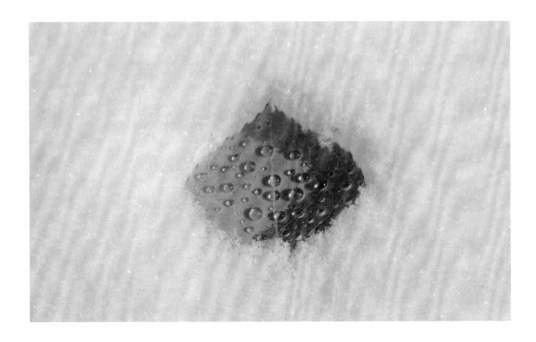

potato salad. Take the time to learn how nature makes colors, and try different things that are the same color such as kumquats, oranges, and carrots, or radishes, tomatoes, and raspberries. Use plant pigments to make paints and dyes for arts and crafts.

SHAPE SHIFTERS

Learn how to make new shapes out of basic forms like triangles, circles, and rectangles. Cut different sizes of the various shapes out of cardboard or wood and put them in a bag. Shake them up and give each player ten shapes. When each player's turn comes along, give him or her sixty seconds to make and name as many objects and shapes as possible to get points. To add a twist, have one player make the shapes and ask a teammate to guess what they are.

6

Motion Motion

Walking down the street, you don't often think about all that it takes to do just that—walk. Consider what it takes for your brain to send a signal to your muscles, for those muscles to react, for your eyes to send more signals to your brain to send to your legs to avoid tripping on the curb. Motion is a complicated thing . . . but it's also as easy as putting one foot in front of the other.

Nature has a way of making difficult things look effortless. Eggs turn into tadpoles and tadpoles into frogs, just like that. Flowers grow from seeds, butterflies migrate thousands of miles. No big deal. But it is. Each of these processes is incredibly complicated and beautiful in its intricacy. Taking the time to understand the effort in the "effortless" is what builds appreciation and wonder for the world.

Wonder comes from awareness, and awareness from understanding. To understand how something works, you often have to take it apart and look at all the pieces. Motion is no different. But taking movement apart isn't as simple as unscrewing the back panel of a clock. Until the invention of photography and the moving image, we couldn't slow movement down enough to really see all the components, to put it under a microscope and look at it frame by frame, step by step. But that doesn't mean we didn't try.

Throughout history, each of the various forms of animation has attempted to understand the intricacies of movement, making animators some of the most knowledgeable individuals on the subject of motion. Looking at the world frame by frame will do that for you. Animators understand the setup, the potential, the release of energy, and the completion of a step—each element as a physiological masterwork. They appreciate the effort that goes into creating movement as they put a frame around each and every stage.

Framing is an important skill. Looking at the big picture is as well, but the big picture is . . . big. It holds everything we can see, as well as everything we can't. When you step back to look at an entire composition, the details can get lost in translation. A blade of grass blends into a meadow. Placing a frame around individual elements brings them back to life. The beauty is in the pieces.

Animation can take many different forms, from simple flip books to feature-length films, but when you break them down, they all start with the same thing: a line. Because of this, learning about movement through animation can be done at any age and any skill level. For the youngest children, it might be just a bouncing ball animated by flipping a stack of scrap paper. Slightly older children may make a zoetrope, and ambitious junior animators might want to make their own magic lantern projector.

FLIP-BOOK ANIMATIONS

Flip books are the simplest and most accessible form of animation. They don't take much in the way of time or materials, and the return on investment is almost instantaneous. A writing utensil paired with a stack of standard printer paper cut in quarters and stapled or sewn along one end is pretty much all you need. Just start drawing pictures, moving them a tiny bit forward on each successive sheet. Soon you'll have a great animation.

One way to reproduce images and keep your animations in line is to use the indentations from each drawing as a register for the next. To do this easily, place a thick piece of paper under the first two sheets of your flip book. Draw your first image, making sure to put enough pressure on the pen to leave an indentation on the sheet below. Once you are finished with the first drawing, move your thick piece of paper back one sheet, and use the indents from the first drawing to help you move your second drawing along a bit. Repeat this process until you run out of pages, and then flip the book!

ZOETROPE

With early variations of the zoetrope dating far back in history, it's safe to say we've been attempting to unlock the secrets of motion for quite some time. A simple spinning apparatus, it uses a series of slits on a rotating cylinder to bring a group of linear images to life, transforming static drawings into moving pictures.

When you rapidly spin an image in a circle, it turns into a blur of colors and unrecognizable shapes. A zoetrope separates each image in the composition to keep this from happening. It puts the focus on each stage of the progression, framing the way you see movement.

Building a zoetrope is a little time-consuming, but once you have the structure complete, you can draw and change the animation anytime you like.

- 1 embroidery hoop, 7" in diameter (found at most craft stores)
- 1 square hard cardboard (like the sturdy back of a drawing pad, at least ⅛" thick) or a piece of thin plywood (found at most craft stores), 10" × 10"
- White glue or wood glue
- 1 wooden dowel, ½" in diameter, 12" in length
- Screw for attaching dowel
- 1 piece white paper, 24" × 3"

- 1 piece black craft paper (medium weight but not so thick that it will crack when bent), 24" × 6"

STEP ONE

Trace the outside of the embroidery hoop onto your cardboard or plywood. Cut out the circle with a pair of scissors (or a jigsaw if you are using wood). Glue the circle to the bottom of the embroidery hoop; take off the outside ring once the inside ring is in place, leaving a little ledge for your circle to sit on. Set this

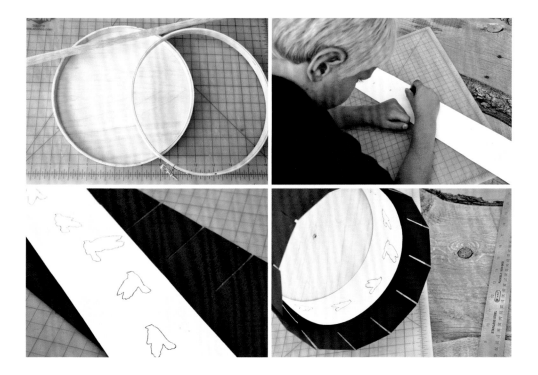

aside and let it dry. Once it is, attach the dowel to the center of the underside of the circle with a screw through the top.

STEP TWO

Starting at the left of one long edge of your white piece of paper, measure across 2¼" and make a vertical line (or simply mark the top edge if you don't want the lines on your animation sheet). From that first line, measure another 2¼" and draw another vertical line. Repeat this process until you have ten "frames." There will be a bit of leftover paper after the last frame, but don't worry about that right now.

Draw a line down the center of the entire length of the black sheet of paper. On the top half (long edge), follow the same process you did for the white sheet of paper, measuring out ten frames.

STEP THREE

With scissors, cut on either side of the vertical lines on the black sheet of paper down to the center line, then between the two to remove about an ⅛" section of paper at each line. Draw your ten-frame animation between each frame (the vertical lines or marks) on the white paper. For the animation to work well, your subject should only move about ⅛" in each frame and should return back to its starting position by the last frame. Please see the animation wheel for the magic lantern on page 212 for an example.

STEP FOUR

Place the larger circle of the embroidery hoop around the smaller circle and slide the black sheet of paper into the space between the circles with the cut side on top. Next, slide the white paper inside of the black sheet, making sure the animations line up in between the cut sections on the black sheet and that the extra paper after the tenth frame goes behind the drawings. Tighten the hoop to hold the papers without having to fasten their ends in any way. Spin your zoetrope between your palms, and watch your animation move!

MAGIC LANTERN

Using many of the same materials required for the zoetrope, you can make a version of a magic lantern, which was one of the earliest forms of projector. This one is slightly different in that the projection isn't outside the device, but it does make quite a nice animation, complete with that old-time film flicker.

- Magic Lantern patterns (see pages 212–213)
- Hard, thin cardboard (like the back of a drawing pad), at least ⅛" thick and large enough to cut out 2 circles, 7" each
- 2 tin cans of the same size, clean, with both ends taken off
- 1 8-32 (or similar) machine screw, 1" in length, with 2 washers and 2 nuts
- Tracing paper
- Glue (regular white glue as well as hot glue or a bit of Super Glue)
- 1 embroidery hoop, 7" in diameter
- Scotch tape
- 1 cork from a wine bottle (also available at craft stores)
- Screws and washers (You will need 4 screws and 2 washers for the apparatus, and then between 2 and 16 screws for your platform, depending on what kind of wood you use. The length of these screws will also depend on your wood, but they should be at least ¼" longer than the thickness of your wood.)
- Enough scrap wood to make an 8" × 16" platform
- Rubber band (for tracing paper over end of can)

- Bendable wire, 14–16 gauge (found near the picture wire at a hardware store)
- 1 lens from a 2× magnifying glass, as big or bigger than the opening of the tin cans
- Flashlight

STEP ONE

Using the patterns provided, cut your front and back pieces for the animation wheel, as well as your shutter top and viewer frame, out of the cardboard. If your tin cans are smaller or larger than the shutter top and viewer frame templates, adjust the diameter of the circles to fit your cans, but keep the slit the same width and the center hole the same diameter. Cut or drill a hole just slightly smaller than the 8-32 screw through the center marks on both the front and back wheels. These are the holes for the pin on which the wheel spins.

On the tracing paper, trace the animation wheel pattern in pencil. You can either draw your own animation inside the small circles or trace the one provided to get the hang of it.

STEP TWO

Glue the front piece of the animation wheel (the cardboard piece with the ten

circular openings) onto the smaller ring of the embroidery hoop (you will not need the outside ring for this project). Also glue the viewer frame to the top of one of the tin cans and the shutter top to the top of the other (with hot glue or Super Glue). Set everything aside to dry.

Now it's time to finish the animation wheel. With a nut and then a washer on the 8-32 screw, push the screw through the front of the animation wheel. Cut out your drawing sequence and put it inside the wheel over the screw (cut an X in the center of the paper to do this). Rotate the animation wheel so that the drawings are centered in the holes and then secure it with a little Scotch tape around the edges.

Cut a piece of cork that is the same thickness as the wheel off the end of the wine cork. Drill or cut a small hole through the center of the cork for the machine screw and place it over the screw on the drawing side of the animation wheel. If you would like to flatten/support your image more, you can add a small cardboard disk between the drawing and the cork (just make sure it doesn't overlap the area where the frames begin).

Working in front of a lamp or other light source, put the back piece of the wheel on (over the machine screw) and rotate it until you can see a line of light through the center of each frame. Secure the back with a nut and washer.

Note: The animation spins on the shaft of the 8-32 machine screw that protrudes beyond the front of the wheel. If you encounter too much friction, or if the wheel wobbles, use the nuts on either side of the wheel to make adjustments forward or backward.

STEP FOUR

With your scrap pieces of wood, make a platform that is roughly 8" × 16". I made mine by cutting two cross pieces to screw the planks to, but you can easily make it from one piece of wood that is 6"–8" wide and 16" long. Basically any sort of platform that will allow you to screw into it will work. I also placed

another thin strip of wood in the center of the platform to elevate the viewing area, but this is completely optional and doesn't change the functionality of the magic lantern in the least if you choose not to include it.

STEP FIVE

Punch a hole (either by predrilling, prescrewing, or using a hammer and nail) in one side of each tin can near the open end about ¼" up from the edge. On the can with the shutter top, make sure the hole lines up at the bottom of the slit in the cardboard top. Take a piece of tracing paper and put it over the shutter end; secure with a rubber band. This will help diffuse the light from the flashlight.

On the can with the viewer frame, put an additional hole on the left and right sides near the open end (the first hole should be at the bottom) about ¼" in from the edge.

STEP SIX

Make an M shape with a 15" piece of the bendable wire (this may require a set of pliers, depending on the pliability of your wire), then bend two circles on each end for the feet (the circles should be big enough to fit your screws and smaller than your washers). Place the tin can with the viewer frame top on the platform with the open end about 1" from the edge of the platform. If you are raising the entire structure with the wood strip, attach it before you do this part. Screw the can down through the bottom hole you punched earlier.

Place your M wire against the back of the can and set the animation wheel in the center of the groove. When you look through the opening of the can in the front, the frame on the back of the can should match up with one of the circle frames on the wheel. You can adjust the height of your M wire by sliding the sides in or out. Once you have it in the right spot, secure it to the platform with a couple of screws and washers through the loop feet.

With the wheel in place, attach the other tin can to the base through the hole you punched earlier, making sure it is close to the wheel without actually touching it.

Twist one end of a 5"–6" piece of wire into a bit of a spiral and put it through one of the holes in the front can from the inside (the spiral functions as a stop). Do the same thing on the other side with another piece of wire. Put the lens at the open end of the can with the viewer frame. Pull each wire across diagonally in front of the lens so the wires make an X, with the center of the X positioned at the top of the lens in the center. Fold the top of the X down behind the lens and secure both sides by wrapping the ends of the wire around the pieces of wire coming out of the holes.

Now just put your flashlight in the open end of the other can and spin the wheel to watch your animation come to life!

PART TWO

Imagination

*If dreams are an open, free association of images, facts,
and emotions, then imagination is a waking dream.*

STRETCHING AND PULLING TOWARD MEANING

It's morning, and the orchestra of sound that usually fills the room is replaced by silence, apart from the occasional bird solo outside. The shadows of early dawn still cover most of the room, except for the window. There, through the old glass panes, a steady stream of sunlight pours in, illuminating everything in its path like a spotlight. Dust that usually falls secretly and silently becomes a constellation of stars floating slowly to the floor. A last fleeting tribute to the changing of the guard; the night is over and the day has begun.

Describing a scene like the one above requires something we all use every day: language. But like most things used on a daily basis, we take for granted the materials and methods of the system itself . . . of what brought it to its current place in our lives and in our speech. Before there was language, the world still existed. There were still forests and mountains and valleys, oceans and waterfalls, but they existed in a singular fashion. They lived in the microcosm of their immediate surroundings. Language makes the world a bigger place. Through description, communication, poetry, and storytelling, the world we can imagine is infinitely more vast than the one we can see, hear, taste, feel, and smell.

In this way, language can be expansive. Language shows us distant lands and long-ago eras. It describes the details of cherry blossoms so perfectly that we can almost touch them. Yet in order to do this, language needs structure. It needs a common foundation on which we can all rely to understand its meaning. It needs words and definitions.

By their nature, definitions *define*. Words take a nebula of sensorial inputs and output a clean, crisp set of letters and sounds. A cluster of cells that grows over a series of decades to form bark, a sturdy trunk, outreaching branches, and sunlight-dappled leaves becomes simply T-R-E-E. In this sense, the words that make up language reduce and contract the very thing they stand for, leaving much for our imagination to fill in.

Expansion and contraction—our perception of the world constantly alternates between these two conditions. We take small words and make big images, and we take big images and make small words. We stretch and pull and reach toward meaning, toward a common understanding. Language allows us all to see similar pictures. It provides a method to contain and categorize a world that would otherwise be far too vast and complex to comprehend. But our real experience exists somewhere in the middle, between perception and definition.[1]

As children, our first pursuit in life is to learn the languages of the world, a process that questions definitions in a way they will never quite be questioned again. Before we understand words, the world is a sensorial playground of free association. Sights, sounds, and smells are connected to each other through somatic experiences, through living and breathing in the world. Everything is what it is at the present moment and has the potential to be something completely different the next. As language begins to define their world, children have to navigate the space between what they perceive and the expansions and contractions of the words that define it. This is the space where I believe our understanding of magic comes from. In the space between perception and language—where children ask questions like, "Can trees talk?" "Can rocks turn into flowers?" or "Can we go to the moon for lunch?"—the functions and boundaries of the world are flexible. Words are just starting points for investigation and inquiry into the exponential tangents of people, places, and things. In the space between perception and definition, our imaginations can take flight.

DAYDREAMING THROUGH IMAGINATION'S LANDSCAPE

When I was a kid, I spent a lot of time daydreaming. At school, at home, in the car, at the park—name the location and you could find me sitting there staring off into the distance. My teachers used to write letters to my parents, concerned that I wasn't "present" during class, that I seemed to be "floating" off somewhere. I always enjoyed school, but in my early years, my attention was split (that is, if you can call 20/80 a "split") between the world I was sitting in and the universe in my mind.

The two worlds weren't vastly different. Many of the same characters could be seen populating the streets of both. But in the world in my mind, the outcome of a given situation would be a far tangent from reality. In my mind, I could start the day going to school and, through a series of complicated interactions, end up in Egypt. In my mind existed the infinite parallel universes for every second I lived. There was no limit to the potential of a moment.

Daydreams are paths and trails through the landscape of imagination. They take cues from the world in front of our eyes and extend them as far as they can reach in our minds, each step revealing another vista just around the bend. Daydreams show us the topography of that landscape. They dig into the dirt of its valleys and pull on the grass of its hills. They show us the depth and breadth of our imagination.

One of the greatest values of exploration is what it teaches us as we find paths and trails to new destinations . . . and make unexpected discoveries along the way. By exploring the landscape of their imagination, children can learn a lot about the potential of the world they are experiencing, as well as the one they want to invent for themselves in the future. Through imagination, children can build boats and sail across the ocean to visit Africa in an afternoon or invent rockets that will take them to the farthest corners of the universe where they can see their favorite stars up close. By investigating the fields and valleys of imagination, children begin to cultivate a desire to make those experiences real, to invent the world of their dreams.

The world as we see it today wouldn't exist if it weren't for the active imaginations of innovators and inventors. If it weren't for the influence of the world of fantasy, we wouldn't live, interact, travel, or communicate the way we do. Reality needs fantasy to support its growth. But likewise, fantasy relies on the real world for inspiration. It's an engine that's built to run, but it won't start without an ignition. Imagination is the key. It lives in the space in between, oscillating from fantasy to reality and back, challenging each to be a little more like the other.

As an adult, I find the split between my focus on the real world and the one that exists in my mind has shifted the other direction to 80/20. But in that 20 percent, I can still find the space of my childhood. I can still find the fields of my imagination.

FILLING IN THE SPACES IN BETWEEN

I've always loved road trips. As a young child, our primary method of vacationing was to pack the whole family (four kids, two adults, and often, a couple of dogs) into the car and head out onto the open road. Each summer we would make the trek from Colorado to Montana to visit family. And even though you would think my parents would want to shorten the "car time" as much as possible (with so many young children in tow), we always took the long road. Two full days of moving landscape outside the window.

There were the traditional sibling squabbles and unexpected restroom breaks off the side of two-lane highways. The spilled drinks and temper tantrums that mark the tableau of American family travel, but then there were the moments when everything got quiet. When we each settled into our current activity, into moving wheels and dotted highway lines, into the space in between.

I would use this time to imagine narratives to go with the scenes I was witnessing outside the car window. When you're in a car moving from one location to the next, your physical relationship to the environment you're moving through is ephemeral. Before you can even take in the shapes of the landscape outside, they've transformed into something else. Your image of the world is in constant flux. I would see myself as a million different characters in as many diverse scenarios. I would test my ideas of who I might be and what I might do in the future. In the space in between, I found the lab of my childhood.

Everyone needs a lab—a place where you can test your hypotheses and experiment with different materials. Where you can make decisions and choices on the routes you want to follow and the topics you want to study. Children's labs are portable; their lab is their imagination. It's the space in between where they are and what they see and possibilities of who they may become. Like the images outside the car window, a child's world is also in flux. It's changing and adjusting to accommodate for knowledge and experience. Imagination will always have new narratives to match the passing scenes, new tests and experiments to help determine the best roads to travel.

Between language and perception. Between fantasy and reality. Between stepping out onto the road and getting where you're going. Imagination is the *in between*—it is childhood. Floating, forming, unforming, landing, and taking off again. It's the only space where you can be, feel, and experience everything in the entire universe while still remaining one simple and intrinsically beautiful thing . . . a kid.

7

Silhouettes on Stage

Five lines and a circle make a man. A couple of zigzags form mountains. One line and you have the horizon. It doesn't take much to call the world to mind. Children's drawings are like that, beautiful and efficient. No fuss with shading or perspective, just exactly what's needed to set the stage. Minimalism at its best.

The reason simple drawings and symbols work is that we already know the pictures they represent so well. Just the slightest trigger and we can see it. From city planning to advertising, many disciplines use this concept, but the theater takes particular advantage of it. Yes, there are lush, opulent sets that leave no detail to the imagination. But then there are the simple ones—the best ones, in my opinion—that ask viewers to complete the image on stage in their imagination, that transport the audience to a new world with a single, well-lit table.

Whereas symbols bring an image to mind, theatrical sets take you there. It's not that they have a higher ability to conjure environments than symbols or drawings do; it's that the actors are interacting with the props, playing with the landscape. Rather than ask you to simply imagine something in your mind based on a visual trigger, a play asks you to be there. A blue sheet ripples on the floor, and you're near the ocean. A tree bough floats in from the left, and you're in an orchard. Imagination and play combined can make things real.

Props and backdrops are like silhouettes, perfect in likeness in one respect and completely open-ended in another, shadows of a million different possible spaces and places. Like shapes in the passing clouds, they create a canvas for imaginative exploration that can be formalized in many different ways, depending on the influences of the day or a particular interest. Playing with these sorts of objects allows children to project the world as they see it exactly in that moment and change it just as easily the next. It allows them to transport the theater of their imagination into the world in front of their eyes.

TREE SHADOWS

Few elements have more theatrical potential than a grouping of trees. The way the light moves through the leaves, the depth of field they create, the shadows they cast. A million stories can come from there. The forest is nature's original stage. Yet not all of us have access to the woods at any given moment. We take advantage of them when we're there, but visits to that sort of larger-than-life, nature-based, magical play can be more infrequent the rest of the time. Unless that is, you can bring the forest to your home.

In the same way that a simple prop can conjure a different world, theatrical backdrops can take you there. Especially when they are shadow drawings of real trees with every bump and crooked branch, every dappled leaf, transposed onto canvas and brought indoors to visit anytime you wish. The forest of your days can become the world of your dreams, a rainy-day haven . . . the beginning of countless adventures.

Shadows replicate life in their own unique way. Simplifying the world into silhouettes, they let go of precision while holding on to character. They render gestures of reality in a quick, efficient manner without losing the nature of their source. Because of this, they are fantastic shapes for budding little artists to copy. In this project, children transfer tracings of tree shadows onto fabric to make theatrical room dividers/backdrops.

MATERIALS

- 1 roll brown craft paper, 34"–36" wide (found at hardware stores in the paint department)
- Pencil, crayon, or marker
- Exacto knife or scissors
- Painter's tape
- Canvas or muslin (2 yards per panel)
- Small foam paint roller
- Fabric or acrylic paint
- Needle and thread or sewing machine
- Ribbon of your choice or string for hanging the panels
- Dowels/rods for hanging panels (optional)

tend to be a bit on the smaller side, so you can fit a little of the trunk and the branches on a sheet of paper.

Once you have found the tree you'd like to trace, pull out a long section of paper from your roll and lay it in the path of the shadow. Morning is a great time to do this, as the shadows are not too long yet. Using a pencil, crayon, or marker, trace the shadow of the tree on the paper. The sun moves faster than you might think, so if you would like an accurate copy of the shadow, you'll have to work relatively quickly. But don't worry, even if the shadow happens to move, the shapes will still work quite well.

STEP ONE

The trick to this project is finding a good tree, where the shadows of the branches are clearly defined. These trees

STEP TWO

Once you have your tracings, it's time to cut out the shapes. This can be done with either an Exacto knife (parents only) or a pair of scissors. While cutting out the shape, note that you can use both the positive and negative pieces to make your theatrical backdrops, so it's good to cut a clean line that leaves both sides in good condition.

Now it's time to decide if you would like to use the positive or the negative of the tree shadow. If you use the positive (the piece of paper that looks exactly like the shadow), you will get a negative image of the tree—meaning the tree shape will be white canvas, and the space around it will be your painted color. If you would like the tree image to be in your paint color, then you have to use the negative of the shadow (the pieces you cut out that go around the tree shape).

Once you've made your decision, you can use painter's tape in a few spots to tape the stencil on your canvas or muslin pieces (you'll have to move the tape as needed to paint under it).

STEP FOUR

Using the foam roller, paint the exposed fabric in the color of your choice. It's important not to put too much paint on the roller, as it will push its way under the stencil. If you keep just a bit of paint on the roller, the process is a lot easier. You can also get texture by painting on top of wood floors (which is what we did for the Tree Shadows pictured here). Texture is a great thing for trees. Play around with the positive and negative of the stencil. Use different painting techniques to develop texture, and by all means, play with color!

STEP FIVE

Once the painting is done and the panels are dry, remove the paper stencils. If carefully rolled and stored, these stencils can be used again. If you happen to have any floating pieces (small sections of stencil that fit inside the open space), it can be a good idea to number them before rolling them up.

There are a number of different options for finishing the room dividers. You can sew a dowel pocket at the top and bottom of each panel, then tie string to both sides of the top dowel and hang them that way. You can do the same thing with a curtain rod in the pocket instead of a dowel and use your backdrops as curtains. You can also fold over and sew the top and bottom edges to finish them (the sides are selvage, so you need not finish them unless you prefer to) and then add a ribbon tab at each corner so you can attach a string. You can even attach long ribbons to the top and use those to tie them up. Choose whichever option seems like the best fit for your space. Now all that's left is to play!

SUGGESTED ACTIVITIES
Outside

The great thing about this project is that the opportunities for fantasy play don't start once the project is complete; they actually begin the moment you step out the door and initiate your search for the right tree. To bring a little of the magic of the forest home (whether your forest is a small group of trees at the park or thousands of acres), you need to understand what that magic feels like. So exploring, running through the trees, and lying on your back to stare at the shifting leaves are all necessary research (kids have great jobs, don't they?). It can also be good to take a little time while you're there to make up stories and think up ideas for plays—anything that can serve as a tether to those moments in the dappled sunlight once you return home.

The time spent drawing the actual shadows can also be a wonderful opportunity to talk about trees and get to know them. Before sitting down to draw, you might take a look at the different trees, identify which species they are, feel their bark, and look for animals that call them home. Which trees are your favorites? Why? How tall do you think one of them is? How long do you think they've been there? Drawing shadows can easily turn into a great lesson in dendrology.

Inside

When the crafting is done and the backdrops are functional, the real theatrical antics can begin. From full-length plays to rainy-day, quiet reading times, the shadow panels can provide the setting for almost anything. They can be forts, shadow puppet theaters, or the forest from *A Midsummer Night's Dream.*

The panels themselves are really just a stepping-off point for a world of fantasy and imagination. A terrestrial staircase to an immeasurable universe of possibility. In short, they're a lot like the trees that inspired them.

8

Under the Stars

The air was cool, but I was warm inside my sleeping bag, with it pulled up to my chin and cinched tight. Each time I moved, it would set off a symphony of nylon, so I made sure to stay as still as possible. As a child, I didn't normally like the dark. I would run up the stairs at home to get to the light switch as quickly as possible, chased by monsters in the shadows. But right then, in my sleeping bag, I loved it. It was different. Instead of obscuring my ability to see, the darkness was letting me see; it was making the stars bright.

Out in the middle of the field, I was the only one still awake; everyone else had long since fallen asleep. Occasionally I would hear them shift and move, breaking the silence for a second before it rushed back in. For that moment, I would be drawn back to the field, but as soon as the quiet returned, I was in the sky. Connecting the dots from one star to the other. Finding constellations and playing out the stories I'd learned in mythology. Losing myself in my imagination. . . .

Since that night, I've always loved camping. The way it makes the world both larger and smaller at the same time. The way you can see both the entire universe and only as far as your flashlight reaches. Life is simple when you're in a tent. There are no work deadlines or algebra tests. There are no bills to pay or errands to run. It's just food, shelter, and adventure. Everything goes into making sure those three simple things are taken care of, and simple is good.

Away from the woods, there are a lot more than three things to think about. Growing up, there were lots of kids in my family. Four to be exact, not counting the other children who lived with us from time to time. And the animals—there were plenty of those too. Needless to say, it was a busy place, our house. As much as the hustle and bustle was fun, there were times when I just needed a little corner of my own, a space where I could feel like I did in the field that night.

When compiling a list of children's needs, "quiet space" doesn't often make the top five. Food, shelter, love, attention, and education normally occupy those spots. But space holds all those concepts up; it supports the work they do. As much as they need to be held close, children also need to inhabit their own worlds. Worlds filled with the narratives of their imagination, with the quiet of their thoughts. They need space to reflect on all they encounter in a day, room to dream about what they'll do the next. We all do.

As a child, I could always find that space in the simple structure of a tent. Even though I couldn't just run to the woods on a whim, I could still go "camping" anytime I wanted. All I needed was a little shelter fashioned from a piece of cloth and some string. Add a flashlight, and I had my ticket back to the quiet, beautiful world of stars and dreams, of camping in the woods.

PLAY TENTS AND STRUCTURES

Anyone who has made a blanket fort at one time or another knows that tents can take many forms. They can be simple and efficient, or they can be multiroom, ornate structures with windows and doors.

As much as I loved my blanket forts as a kid, I always bemoaned their fragility, the delicate balance of quilts, book stacks, and dining room chairs that threatened to fall at any given moment. No matter how much I tried, they would eventually and inevitably fall apart. If only I had known how to sew, it would have been a completely different story. In this chapter, you will find a few suggestions for sewing and constructing tents that can handle all of the make-believe you can throw their way.

TENT OPTION ONE

This first tent option is really just a glorified bedsheet, but in the best possible way. It has the ability to change its shape the way a regular blanket fort can; it's lightweight and portable like a bedsheet; but it has one key difference: rigging. With a few ribbon loops and a little rope, your tent will withstand the winds of play any day.

MATERIALS

- Flat bedsheet (size of your choice)
- 1 roll ribbon, 1" wide
- Needle and thread or sewing machine
- Clothesline
- Fabric paint (optional)

STEP ONE

Lay out your bedsheet and decide where you would like to place your ribbon ties. I would make sure to have loops at the four corners, but you could also attach loops between them along the sides, as well as along the center line of the sheet. A few additional loops placed in random locations might end up making interesting shapes later.

STEP TWO

To make ribbon loops for your ties, simply cut 16" pieces of ribbon and finish the cut edges by folding the ends over twice and sewing them in place. Then fold the ribbon ties in half and make a small loop (about 2") by crossing one ribbon over the other so there is an X shape where they cross. Sew back and forth over the center of each X until they are secure. This makes loops that you can run clothesline through, or you can use the loose ends of the ribbons to tie the sheet directly to an object.

To make loops that don't have ties, simply cut 4" pieces of ribbon, fold them in half, and sew the ends together about ½" from the edge. Flip the loops inside out so the seam is on the inside.

STEP THREE

Now that you have your ribbon loops, sew them to the sheet in the places you selected in step one. If you are using the loops with ties, attach them so that the ties are hanging over the edges of the fabric with the loops above. Make sure to really secure each tie well. If you like, you can even reinforce the fabric where you are going to attach the loops by sewing patches of heavy fabric there first or by ironing on pants patches and then sewing through both layers of fabric at the junction of the loop. For the loops without ties, attach them with the seam against the sheet.

STEP FOUR

Now that your tent structure is complete, you can set it up right away by running pieces of clothesline through the loops and/or tying them to tables, doorknobs, dresser drawers, trees, bushes, and so on, or you can decorate it with fabric paint first and set off on your adventures once it is dry.

TENT OPTION TWO

If you would like a tent that is freestanding, then a simple wooden structure can be made to support your tent fabric. This takes a bit more time to make and a few tools, but once it's set up, it can be used over and over again.

MATERIALS

- 2 pieces of wood, 2" × 2" × 8'
- 2 pieces of wood, 1" × 2" × 8'
- 2 bolts, ¼" in diameter, 3½" long

- 16 washers
- 8 wing nuts
- 4 eye screws with ¼" eyes
- Clothesline, ¼" in diameter, or strong rope
- 6 bolts, ¼" in diameter, 2½" long

STEP ONE

Cut your 2" × 2" × 8' pieces of wood in half so you have four 4' pieces. You can do this with a handsaw or a power saw (but only if you know how to use one well). Then cut your 1" × 2" × 8' pieces in half so you again have four 4' pieces; for this project, you will need only three of them. For the feet of the tent (the 2" × 2" stock) to rest flat on the ground, you need to cut them at a 32.5-degree miter. This is a standard stop on a chop saw, but you can also draw it with a protractor and cut it with a handsaw. Cutting the feet at this angle makes the tent a bit more stable, but it isn't necessary. It will still stand with a straight 90-degree cut as well.

STEP TWO

Measure down 4" from one end on each of the 2" × 2" pieces and drill a ¼" hole all the way through the center of the wood. Next, measure up 4" on the opposite end

of each piece, on the side faces of the sticks (the opposite face from where you just drilled); drill a ¼" hole all the way through.

Measure ¾" down from each end of each of your 1" × 2" pieces and drill a ¼" hole all the way through the center of the wood on the 2" face. Each piece will have a hole in both ends.

STEP THREE

Take two of the 2" × 2" pieces and cross the left piece over the right one so the holes you drilled earlier line up. Fasten them together using a 3½" bolt, two washers, and one of the wing nuts (with the nut on the back). Now do the same thing with the other two pieces, but this time, cross the right piece over the left one and bolt them together (with the nut on the back again). You should now have two A-frames that can expand and collapse.

On the inside face of each leg and ¾" from the bottom, screw in an eye screw. Open your structure to the width you'd like and securely tie one side of your clothesline or rope through one of the eye screws. If you know the exact width you'd like in advance, cut your rope 4" longer than that width and tie the rope through the other eye screw, trimming off any excess. If you want to be able to adjust the width of your A-frame, you can tie an adjustable knot to the second eye screw. Repeat the process for the second A-frame.

STEP FOUR

Now that you have your two ends done, it's time to attach the crosspieces. Expand one of the A-frames and place one of the 1" × 2" pieces inside the X at the top of the frame so that it lines up with the outermost edge of the frame. Make a mark with a pencil through the hole in the 1" × 2" piece onto the wood below. Take the 1" × 2" out and collapse the frame so you can drill a ¼" hole all the way through the side of the 2" × 2" piece where you just made your mark. Repeat this for the other A-frame.

Once the holes are drilled in the frames, use the 2½" bolts with washers and wing nuts to attach the crosspiece. Use the same process to bolt the ends

of the other two 1" × 2" pieces to the outside bottom of each leg through the holes you drilled earlier, as shown in the photo. Your frame is done! Perfect for draping bedsheets and blankets over or for making a tent with doors and windows as in the option that follows.

TENT OPTION THREE

If you want a tent with more bells and whistles, you can make this cover to go with the frame from Tent Option Two.

MATERIALS

- 5 yards canvas or painter's drop cloth, 48" wide
- Tent frame from the previous option
- Sewing machine
- 10 yards cotton webbing, 1¼" wide
- 1 yard cotton muslin
- 1 roll ribbon (width of your choice) for the window and door tiebacks

STEP ONE

Lay your canvas over the tent frame so one end just touches the bottom. Make a mark where the other end meets the ground on the other side. Measure 2" past this mark and cut your canvas to this length. This will be the tent body.

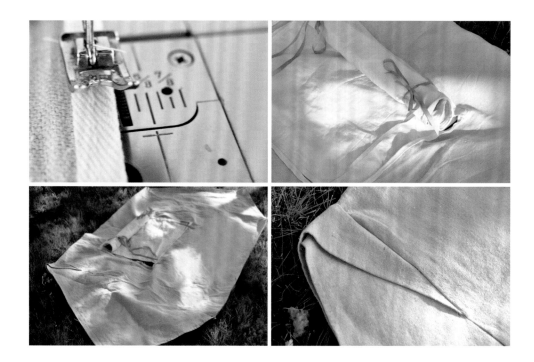

To make the doors, measure the height of the triangle opening from the highest point at the center down to the ground and write down this measurement. Now measure from one corner at the bottom of the A-frame to the other corner, divide that number in two, and note the result. Add 4" to each number that you just wrote down.

Lay out the remaining canvas. Measure out from one corner of the fabric and mark the height (plus those 4") along the length of that side. Mea-

suring from the same corner but in the opposite direction, mark the width (plus the 4") along the cut edge of the fabric. With a straight edge, draw a line between the two points and cut along this line. Repeat this three more times so you have four triangular pieces.

Finish the edges along the two sides of each panel that correspond to the measurements you used to make it by folding them under twice by ½" and sewing them in place (don't finish the diagonal line you cut on).

STEP TWO

Finish the two shorter sides of your rectangular piece by folding the edges under twice by ½" and sewing them in place.

Place one of the triangular pieces on the rectangular piece with the unfinished edges and bottom corners aligned. Sew the pieces together ½" from the edge. Place another triangular piece at the opposite corner on the same side of the rectangle and sew it in place in the same way. Your triangular pieces should overlap at the top by a couple of inches. Repeat on the other side of the rectangle.

STEP THREE

If you want only doors, you can stop at this point and place your cover over the frame. If you would like to add roll-up windows on each side, follow these steps.

Lay your completed tent on the ground, folded in half along the top edge with the doors on either side. Mark where you want to have your window, then use scissors to cut through both layers of the fabric at once to make both windows at the same time. Finish the raw edges of each opening by folding the cotton webbing in half over the edges and sewing it down.

To make the roll-up covers, cut two pieces of canvas that are 2" larger than your openings on all sides and two pieces of cotton muslin to the same dimensions. Layer one piece of muslin and one piece of canvas wrong sides together, sew along the two short sides and one long side ½" from the edge, and turn right side out. Repeat for the other flap.

STEP FOUR

Cut a piece of webbing that is 2" longer than the unfinished side of the window flaps and finish the two ends of the webbing so they won't fray. Turn them under twice by ½" and sew. Cut four 20" pieces of ribbon. Measure 4" in from either side of the unfinished edge of the flap. Fold a ribbon in half over the edge at each measurement so half of the ribbon hangs in front of the flap and the other half hangs in back. Repeat for the other window flap. Place the webbing along the top of the flap, aligning the top edge of the fabric with the center line of the webbing (leave half of the webbing above the edge of the fabric). Sew the webbing and the ribbons to the flap. Place the flaps over the window openings and sew them in place along the webbing. Your tent is now complete!

My Kingdom

The old wooden stairs let out a creak with every step. Hand over foot, I would gallop up them in a few short bounds. This was a risky technique, as the landing midway through the staircase forced me to maneuver a ninety-degree turn at top speed. Any bumps or bruises would quickly be forgotten as I turned the doorknob to my room and flew into my own little universe. Here, dreams rested on the soft folds of stars, moons, and clouds; fairies and gnomes would greet me as I walked through the door.

Time didn't exist here, nor did any rules. Within the walls of my bedroom kingdom, a village lay in various forms of constant rearrangement, its inhabitants busy working at their assigned tasks for the day. It was made up of three wonderful cottages. The first was fairly traditional, with a family of five inhabiting it and trying their hardest to make ends meet. Up the street and around the corner, a tree house gave shelter to the gnomes and fairies who helped the garden out back grow big and bright. And on the far side of the kingdom lay the greatest house of all. Taller than myself, it had living quarters for the kingdom's resident giants named Addy, Josephina, and Molly.

A few feet outside the village walls lay a big, blue, army-style chest, locked up tight with twenty-five cents worth of protection. Tiny keys hidden under a jar of magic fairy dust were the only means of unlocking the magic chest, albeit a bobby pin would do in a pinch. Inside the chest lay costumes—my passports to nearly every country and era in time. Adventures always required a cape, and if the circumstances were dangerous, perhaps a glowing light saber. Of course, grand rescues and capes were not always the order of the day. Invitations to Cinderella's ball required much different attire, and I had the perfect princess dress: a giant white ball gown complete with a lace bodice and a massive puffy skirt.

Adventures would come and go just like grand balls, so in between, I would hone my cooking skills in my tiny galley kitchen. Small in stature, the wooden stove was my favorite. I could make anything—and I mean anything—on that stove. Of course, that meant securing the proper ingredients, which sometimes required a journey outside the kingdom and into the forest. The forest had everything I needed. Mounds of chocolate could be found under any bush or plant, with rock candy strewn throughout the mix. Seasonings such as flowers, greens, and an occasional stick for some earthy flavor were also very important. Once I had all the ingredients, it was back to my kingdom to test new recipes. Messes would inevitably be made, but trial and error was the only way to perfection. And by the end of a day's effort, the whole kingdom would feast together in delight.

Nothing was ever boring in my kingdom; new adventures and dramatic events flowed along with my imagination. In my mind, years would go by without being disturbed, I could grow up and down with the flip of a thought. The world outside this small kingdom could be filled with the chaos of everyday life, but once the door shut behind me, I was safe. My kingdom was a peaceful one filled with animals, people, and all forms of magical creatures. The most important part was that it was mine, the place where my imagination knew no limits, where anything and everything was possible.

—Jordan

9

The Magic of Provenance

When I was growing up, my mom was always telling stories about our family. It could be about my great-grandmother and her upbringing on a rural Montana sheep farm, or it could be a tale about my great-great-great-great-grandmother Florence. My mother loved history and the art of a good story. Being a young child, though, I would often lose focus and simply let the sound of her voice become the musical accompaniment to my play. The stories were interesting (especially hearing them again as an adult—my family has no dearth of good characters), but they were a bit abstract for me then, since they didn't involve people I knew, and those people rarely did things like fight dragons or save the world from evil sorcerers. However, when my mother related the history of objects in our home, you couldn't pry my attention away.

There is something powerful about history when it is embodied in a physical object. Objects have a special weight to them when they come with a story. It's history in a palpable sense—a past you can touch with your fingers rather than an abstract string of words. It's almost as if the item itself contains the entire story related to it, like a portal to the past. Like a wardrobe that opens the door to a parallel world, objects with stories are magical.

To be a kid is to live in the moment, to experience the world as we come into contact with it, one leaf, one bug, one sunny afternoon at a time. As adults, we spend most of our time trying to find that relationship to the present again. For a child, it is connections to the past and future that are tenuous. Objects with stories, with provenance, can strengthen that link.

A ring is just a piece of semiprecious metal until it becomes an Etruscan ring from 700 B.C. Then it is priceless, a piece of a time we will never see again. Wine from a vineyard with a special story is worth more than its contemporaries. A cotton dress worn by Jackie Onassis is not just any ordinary dress. We cherish these things because they connect us to the larger picture of life. They connect us to a larger understanding of ourselves, to the world our life span can't attempt to hold. The same can be said for objects of fantasy for children.

By connecting narratives from history to objects, children can build a strong relationship to the past. By tying fairy tales to real-life objects, they are creating a tether to the magic of childhood. If you can grasp a magic wand in your hand, then the stories it embodies, the enchantment it holds, are real. With them, childhood can never be lost.

WANDS AND OTHER ENCHANTMENTS

If there was ever an object that is a direct tie to the world of magic, it's a wand. Simple or ornate, it makes no difference; the purpose is the same: to transform the world of imagination into reality, to make tangible objects out of dreams and wishes.

This project is more about the process of collecting materials and crafting stories than about time spent gluing and sewing. But making magic is a careful procedure just the same. Magic has to grow from a seed. Just like a plant, it needs energy and nutrients, time and care.

If there is one thing I have learned in my years spent working with and designing for children, it's that their investment in an object or activity is proportional to their participation in its creation. Simply put, when kids make things themselves, they like them more. This couldn't be truer than in the case of magic wands. Every child has his or her own image of what a wand should look like—its size, its color, and its shape. So who better to search out the materials to make one? This could mean a trip to the woods, the park, a store, or even just to the junk drawer. An expedition, however big or small, is definitely in order.

Explorers usually step out the door with a goal in mind, and reaching that goal often takes a bit of preparation. The same is true for wand hunting. In order to find what you're looking for, you have to know what you're looking for. Drawing and writing can be perfect ways to figure that out. Here are a few good questions to help kick-start the process:

- What is it made of?
- What color is it?
- Where do you think it can be found?

- Who do you think we will meet along the way?
- Who else has a wand like this?
- How is the wand made?
- What can it do?

The answers to these questions may be images or stories or both. They may be maps or lists; they may even be songs. But whatever their form, they will leave you with a path to follow.

EXPLORING AND COLLECTING

Where and how you find the pieces of a wand are just as important as the end result. They're the main plot of its story. So it almost goes without saying that collecting them should be a bit of an adventure. Special clothes, a backpack full of "tools and supplies" (a snack, something to write with, a notebook, magnifying glasses, binoculars, and so on) can all help an everyday outing to the park become a magical treasure hunt. Handmade or found bags for collecting materials (pretty much any sort of small cloth bag) can transform sticks and string into precious specimens with enchanted properties. When I was a kid, I remember picking the white stones out of regular pea gravel and calling them

"moonstone." As soon as they had a name—a story—they were magical. The same is true for each of the objects you'll collect while searching out wand materials. The more detailed the process, the more intricate the end story will be. Will the sap from a fallen branch enchant everything it touches? Will a regular old stone shine with the light of a thousand crystals when attached to the top of a wand? Will string woven by elves hold the magic of an entire forest inside one little twig when wrapped around it? Material potential is limitless when you're looking for magic.

MAKING AND STORING

Once you have collected the materials and recorded their stories, the wand will come together rather easily. It may be as simple as wrapping a bit of string around one end of a stick to make a handle, or it may involve paint, stones, and glue—whatever method the wand maker deems best at the moment. But a wand isn't complete without a safe place

to keep it and all the stories that come with it, a way to hold the memories and magic, the remnants of a day in childhood.

Whether it's a simple bag or an ornate box, the container that holds the wand is just as important as the tool itself. Wooden boxes can be painted or decorated with wood-burning tools and intricate patterns, or they can be simple and unassuming on the outside with a lush velvet lining on the inside. Maybe the container is not a box at all; perhaps it's a bag. Maybe there's a handwritten message sewn into the lining from the wizard who previously owned it. Whatever its form, a special tool deserves an equally beautiful place to call home.

Last, but certainly not least, is to come up with a method or place to keep the stories and the history of the wand, those gathered during its creation, as well as the ones that are yet to be written. While they can simply remain loose in the wand's storage bag or box,

binding them into a book or making a special hard folder can protect those precious tales from falling apart over the years. That way when the little wizards grow up to have their own magical brood, they may be able to pass some of the enchantment down to the next generation.

10

By the Sea

Innovation has never been an exact science; in fact, I'd say it is pretty much the opposite. It's more like trial and error or even, in some circumstances, pure luck. Yet if there is one thing all innovators have in common, it's that they see a future that isn't yet possible, and it doesn't stop them from trying to get there . . . even if it means making their own transportation.

Early boatbuilders were first-rate innovators. Standing at the shores of vast oceans and seas, they dared to think that something existed beyond the horizon and that, with a little hard work, they could build a vessel to take them there. In today's world, it's difficult to even imagine how large a feat that was. With global satellite imaging and instruments like the Hubble telescope, even space can't hide from our view. We have equations and algorithms to calculate the gravity of another planet and the thickness of its atmosphere. We can make educated guesses and build complex machines to take us to new territories.

Before all that technology, making a leap into the unknown was a different story. It lived more in the imagination than in equations. Early explorers relied on intuition and observation to help them see the world more clearly. Childhood inhabits the realm of early exploration. Kids don't yet know how everything works or what it looks like, so each day, they take that leap into the unknown. They trust their instincts and move forward. If they fail, they learn to try another method. If they succeed, they build the confidence to leap again.

Humans are capable of a lot of things, but swimming for thousands of miles at a stretch and gliding through the air unassisted are a little out of our skill set. So instead, we do what we do best. We learn from observation. We look for elements in the world that can perform those tasks and try to copy their actions. How do birds fly? How do fish swim? What materials approximate a bird's wing? What materials float in water? Nature has had a lot of time to test things out and is perhaps the best expert when it comes to the science of materials.

Innovation is made up of observation and experimentation, two concepts embedded in the fibers of childhood. Children are born innovators. They wake up, take the world in, and try to learn its ways, all while making their own. Each moment, they stand at the edge of that great ocean and wonder what lies just beyond it. They have all the right skills to make the leap to a new world; all they need is the space and time to work it out.

BOATS FOR SAILING IMAGINARY SEAS

Every innovation is inspired by curiosity, by a desire to see a place or an object that, up to this point, has only lived in the realm of imagination. A curiosity to see the other side of the horizon is what inspired much of the innovation that has brought us the ships of the past and the present. So it's safe to say that cultivating a healthy curiosity in children for what lies just around the bend could be a direct route to navigating the seas of the future. Building boats for the imagination can be a good way to kick this off.

Whether they're made of sheets and clothespins, logs and cloth sails, or sticks and string, boats for imaginary play can lead to real-world aspirations for travel, adventure, engineering, and innovation. They can take you to far-off lands and immerse you in the winds and salty mists of the sea . . . right from your own backyard.

Of all the elements of nature, water is one of the best proving grounds for good design. Whatever you make will either sink or float. It will glide on the surface or slowly fall below it, but all along the way, there's room for adjustment, problem solving, and innovation. Water makes you think on your feet, so you can move effortlessly through the waves.

In this chapter, you will find a few suggestions for building different types of boats as well as some experiments with materials and techniques. Hopefully, these will be just the beginning of much more.

First and foremost, to float on top of water, you need to keep it from coming into your boat. Playing with different materials to test their imperviousness to water will help you decide how to choose the material you'd like to use to build your boat or what you need to add to the materials you already have.

One easy way to tell if a material is waterproof or water-resistant is to drip some water onto its surface. If the water stays on top in the form of little drops, then it is at least water-resistant. Wood and other natural materials are water-resistant, since their fibers swell and get tighter together when wet. Yet when submerged in water for a long period of time, wood will eventually get water-logged and sink, so it needs a little help to seal it off.

In modern boat making, there are lots of different polymers and complex sealants that keep a boat watertight, but for the sake of experimenting with kids, a little wax is all you need. For a direct example of the power of sealants, simply drop a bit of water onto a piece of paper and see what happens. Then, with a different sheet, put some heated wax on paper and let it cool prior to the dripping the water on it. Do you notice anything different? After playing with materials to see how they are affected by the sealant, try making a basic paper boat with untreated paper and then with waxed paper. How well do they sail?

Since I was a kid, I've always loved paper boats, but their life is an ephemeral one at best. They can sail puddle seas and creek waves for only so long until they turn into a soggy mass of wet pulp. If you seal them, they can go on many more adventures before their time is up.

FLOATING

Perhaps one of the most entertaining parts of boatbuilding is testing materials for their buoyancy and learning about the displacement of water. Objects float in water when the weight of fluid they push out of the way (displace) is greater than the weight of the object itself.[1] Certain formulas can guide you to the exact figures you need to make a boat float, but I've always found that the best way to begin learning about concepts in math and science is through experimentation.

To experiment with materials and

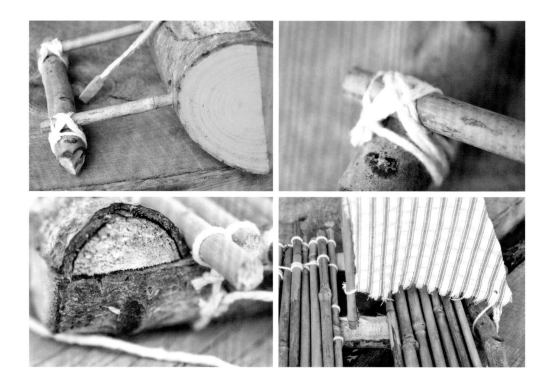

displacement, all you need are two containers (a small transparent glass and a big bucket); some water; and a bag full of different materials (from sticks and thin, wide, wooden scrap pieces to recycled milk jugs and yogurt tops—anything that is watertight or water-resistant). For a clear and easy way to understand how objects move water around, take the small transparent glass and fill it halfway with water; place a piece of tape at the waterline. Take a handful of stones,

marbles, or coins and gently drop them in the glass; place another piece of tape at the new waterline. The objects have moved (displaced) the water by the difference in the two lines. The volume of water added happens to be exactly the same volume of stones, marbles, or coins you added to the cup.

Now for the really fun part (especially if it happens to be a warm summer day and you're out in the backyard). With your bag of water-resistant materials and big bucket of water at the ready, answer these questions about each material and don't hesitate to make up some of your own!

- Does it float or sink?
- If it does float, how long will it stay up?
- If it floats, can it carry weight?
- If it can carry weight, how much will it hold? (Try using things like pennies or buttons that are all the same size and weight to test this.)
- Which floats better, small objects or big objects? Small objects that are light or heavy? Larger objects that are light or heavy?
- Try putting in an empty plastic bottle. What happens? Fill the plastic bottle with water. What happens then?

Hint: If your boat isn't holding enough weight for your liking, you can make the sides taller or the bottom wider; both of these additions will increase the available volume of water your boat can displace.

Fun Fact: Whatever the boat weighs, it must displace exactly that same weight in water. Fortunately for us, water is very heavy (as compared to many other materials), which is why giant boats made of steel or concrete can actually float. We know that water weighs roughly eight pounds per gallon, so a ship that weighs 100,000 pounds must displace 12,500 gallons of water! A small boat that you might make will weigh perhaps a pound, so it will only need to displace an eighth of a gallon of water. You can even calculate how much your boat weighs by measuring the volume of water it displaces (like you measured the two waterlines) and multiplying that volume by the density of water (eight pounds per gallon).

FINDING BALANCE

All these experiments can help a child learn, in a somatic way, how objects float and what shapes and sizes work best. The log boat pictured is a good example of playing with shape and weight as it relates to buoyancy and balance.

A solid log will often float, but it will also roll and be a bit arduous to maneuver. Also, it can be a little hard to stay on top of. As much as a boat needs to float and be watertight, it also needs to be balanced. If a boat isn't balanced, it could roll or topple over. An easy way to illustrate this is by asking children to stand on one leg. Ask them to lean a little to the left and then a little to the right, back and forth, until they have to put their other foot down for balance. The support of their other foot is what keeps them from toppling over.

For a boat the "other foot," or stabilizing element, can be a number of things. One element that is often used is an outrigger (a rigid hull attached to the main boat to provide stability and to keep it from capsizing). This log boat has an outrigger for exactly that reason.

Without it, the boat would roll around, eventually fill with water, and sink. With it, the boat can easily stay on the surface.

WIND

Paddleboats, such as the log boat, move forward on the power and persistence of their operator. Yet if there is one element that is nearly always present around large bodies of water, it's wind, which is exactly why boats have been taking advantage of this means of pro-

pulsion for centuries. Sails, along with their power and efficiency, make boat-building a completely new ball game. Wind is such a strong force that the shape and size of a sail, along with its position, can power a boat alone. So why not try out a few different options and see what happens? On a simple stick raft try out a triangular sail attached to a fixed point, a triangular sail with a boom, and a rectangular sail.

- For the fixed triangular sail (see photo on page 114), simply cut a triangular piece of cloth and attach it to the top and bottom of the mast. Fix the third corner to a point on the back of the raft directly behind the mast.
- For the triangular sail with a boom, attach the first two corners of the sail to the mast in the same way, but then attach a wooden stick to the bottom

of the sail. Make a few different spots to tie it off at the back of the raft (when attached perpendicular to the boat, the boat can sail downwind— the direction of the wind—quite rapidly).

- For the rectangular sail, attach two crosspieces to the mast—at the top and bottom—with a little string, then attach the rectangular sail to these pieces.

How do the sails work differently? In which direction do the boats move with each of the different sails? What happens when you move the triangular sail from left to right?

These initial steps into the world of boatbuilding are exactly that—first steps. There's an ocean of possibility out there and a million different ways to sail it. Why not try them all?

Leaves and Boats

Deep in the woods, somewhere in Maine, a small, red Volkswagen Beetle crawled its way up a narrow gash of dirt road. It was fall and far from anywhere. The Beetle opened its wings and delivered a young couple and their first child into a sublime landscape of fallen maple leaves framed by the trees from which they'd come. In front of them stood an old cabin, and inside awaited the gazes of the dearest and oldest of friends. The day began with breakfast and brownie baking. At midday, the couple stepped out for a walk in the woods, leaving their child in good hands with the gazes that had found their eyes earlier. The young woman took a moment with her son, sat him down, and proceeded to explain that she and his father would be leaving briefly, but upon their return, they would deliver the most gorgeous of toy boats for him to play with in the brook below. His eyes and mind widened, and for the next few hours, he painted glorious images of his fantastic new boat in his mind. It was red and shiny with three smokestacks proudly standing in a row. Full with these images and heavy with sleep, the little boy slipped into a slumber warmed by late afternoon sunbeams and the smell of freshly baked brownies.

The little boy awoke to the familiar shape of his mother's face as she smiled at him and asked if he was ready for his brand-new, glorious boat and promised that it would be the best of its kind in all the world. His imagined construction of the boat flashed once more in his still-dreamy head. "Close your eyes, and hold out your hands," his beautiful mother instructed.

So he did. But what should have been the heavy thump of a sturdy toy boat was replaced by something light and delicate. To his shock and dismay, what lay in his palms was a giant maple leaf!

"This is your new toy boat! Isn't it beautiful? It was made just for you."

The young child looked at his mother, sad and confused.

She saw the look on his face and said, "It may not look like a normal boat, but take it down to the creek and see how well it floats and moves like a boat."

So the boy reluctantly took his "boat" down to the creek and cried the entire way, mourning the loss of his imagined boat that somehow got swapped out for a big, dumb leaf. *This is not a boat! It's a leaf!* The boy felt betrayed and threw the leaf into the creek.

The leaf sailed through the air like a glider and set down in the creek like those seaplanes the boy had seen on TV. It caught a small eddy in the creek, spun around, banked, shot over a rock, jumped into the air, and splashed back down into the water with such attitude that the boy fell instantly in love with his amazing new toy—no longer a leaf but a beautiful boat given to him by his wise young mother. Maple leaves were never leaves to the boy again. The mother had forever transformed them into gorgeous, swift-moving boats made just for him.

—*Noah*

11

In the Spotlight

We all know what the world looks like through our own eyes. We judge new situations based on past experiences and see our environment through the same filter. But what happens when we look at things through someone else's eyes? How will their experiences affect our own perception? How will the way they see trees and clouds, hills and valleys, affect the way we see them? The beauty of role play is that it allows you to do exactly that.

Children are constantly role-playing to some extent or other. As they are developing their own personalities, they try on the ones nearest to them. They copy mannerisms, phrases, likes, and dislikes to find their own predispositions. Some of this happens during mundane daily activities, and some of it happens during play. But it all goes to the same end: understanding the world and themselves. Fantasy play has a lot to do with reality.

Growing up, I attended a school that treated every lesson as an opportunity to tell a great story. Whether it was math, science, or history, there were beautiful drawings and dramatic tales to bring the lessons to life. Hard facts and mythology shared the same delivery system. I was introduced to Napoleon through the same chalk that illuminated the Pythagorean theorem. Through the theater of history, I learned about the drama of the everyday, and through the drama of the everyday, I learned about the power of the theater.

Theater creates a universe where the laws, principles, and rules of the world are blurred. Simple equations no longer exist in the vacuum of $x = 4$. Instead, they mix and mingle with images and stories, life and dreams, reality and fiction. Scenes from the everyday can appear, or dragons can swoop down from the rafters. A stage has the power to let any story make its way to the forefront, no matter how big or small. Giving children control of the players lets them write the script.

As adults, we are constantly categorizing thoughts, activities, and emotions in order of importance. Time and experience have taught us it is necessary to do this. Simply too many things happen in a given day to discuss each and every one. And too few people would like to hear about them all. So we often lose the stories about spring birds that made us smile or songs on the radio that made us sad. Instead, they become threads in the fabric of our daily lives—lost in a pattern that contains a million others just like them.

For kids, every story is important; there's no hierarchy. Their only challenge is to find a place to tell them all. I've heard epic tales about worms on the sidewalk. Hilarious comedies starring a squished peanut butter and jelly sandwich. Action thrillers centered around the walk from school to the park. Each and every one filled with drama and excitement (as well as a lot of "and then" . . . "and then" . . . "and then" . . .).

A stage is the democratic home of storytelling, with equal rights for every voice. It replicates the freedom and space of being a kid, and it's the perfect place to act out the theater of the everyday. To bring each and every beautiful detail of childhood to the place it belongs: in the spotlight.

NATURE'S MARIONETTES

Puppets have been made out of found materials for a long time, much longer than the years I've spent on this planet. When I was a kid, I made them out of everything from old socks to paper lunch bags. Somehow the use of found materials made the puppets all the more enchanting, as though they had appeared out of thin air. Or better yet, as though my own personal brand of magic brought them to life. With these simple marionettes made from natural found materials, not only is there the magic that comes from making objects with your own hands, but there is also the vast and beautiful magic of Mother Nature.

The construction will be a bit different for each marionette, since the materials will differ depending on what you collect. So instead of a straightforward how-to, this section will give you various techniques for attaching different materials and making movable joints. Then, depending on your materials, you can choose the options that best match what you have in front of you.

MATERIALS

- String
- Picture wire
- Small eye hooks
- Sticks, pinecones, dried moss, bark, stones, dried fungi, and so on
- Hot glue gun (optional)
- Cloth (optional)
- Thread (optional)
- Wooden beads (optional)

MAKING JOINTS

The most important elements on a marionette are the joints. They are what give it its character and its personality. Here are a couple of options for making movable joints.

Eye Hooks

The simplest method I've found for making fluidly moving joints is with tiny eye hooks. Easily found at your local hardware store, you can screw them by hand

into the ends of sticks and the like, then just use a bit of picture wire or thread to connect the two "eyes."

Cloth

There may often be multiple types of joints on one puppet, frequently with cloth used to construct the arms. Cloth provides an extremely expressive arm/hand movement to which other materials cannot come close. You can easily connect cloth arms or legs to the body by sewing them to eye hooks that have been attached to the body or by wrapping thread around the body while sewing through the cloth. To construct cloth arms, you can simply cut a piece of cloth to the length and width you desire, or you may cut your fabric slightly larger so you can finish the edges by folding them over and sewing them in place. In either case, I suggest placing a wooden bead or something a little heavier than the cloth on the ends of the arms to make

the hands. This allows the marionette's arms to drop and swing in that characteristic way we all love.

Note: For the arms on the marionettes pictured here, I sewed only one long section of cloth and wrapped it around the back of the pinecone. Then I sewed through the middle of the arms and wrapped my thread around the pinecone between each stitch. Almost how you would attach a button (with the pinecone as the button).

MAKING THE BODY

The body of a marionette can be constructed of many different materials, but it must be made of a material that allows for connections and joints for the arms and legs. I've listed a couple of suggestions here.

Pinecones

Depending on the material you choose for your body, you will have different options for attaching the appendages and the head. For the marionettes pictured here, I really enjoyed using pinecones for the body portions—not only because they were abundant and lightweight, but also because their many layers provided an easy way to attach the other components. I was able to attach the "wings" by poking holes in the dried fungi and threading simple picture wire through them and around the pinecone bodies. I used the same technique for attaching the legs.

Sticks

If you want to use a large stick for the body, I suggest using the eye hook and picture wire method described earlier for attaching the arms and legs. Or you can drill a small hole through the stick to pass your thread, string, or picture wire through.

Other Materials

Since these marionettes are meant to be fairly free-form, you can really make the body out of any material that can be attached to the arms and legs. My only suggestion is that you use a material that supports mechanical connections (sewing, eye hooks, and so on), because glue joints will most likely fall apart rather easily around the movable parts.

We've covered the arms, legs, and body, so now all that's left are the head and the feet. For these, I've found that a simple fixed solution works well. For the marionettes pictured here, I simply hot glued the mini-pinecones I used for my head and feet, but if you are using a wooden bead for the head and a stick for the body, you could also screw the head on through a hole in the bead. Likewise, if you are using sticks for the feet, you can glue them or attach them with a small screw so they remain perpendicular to the legs.

SUGGESTED ACTIVITIES

- Nature walks or family hikes are a great way to gather materials for the marionettes and to talk about where each piece you pick up comes from and what its function is in nature. For example, when collecting a pinecone, you might talk about how plants make seeds and how those seeds travel from the plant to other locations. Looking for stones can be a great way to initiate a discussion about geology or to identify rocks. Every object is an opportunity for investigation.
- Since the materials are to be made

into marionettes for dramatic play, it can be fun to make up stories about the parts and pieces and the locations where you found them. A crystal may be a magical crystal that becomes a good wizard puppet. A pinecone may be the daughter of the forest king and turn into a princess marionette. The place where you find a stick might be the enchanted forest that the stage represents.

- Children can use quiet time or rainy-day time to draw storyboards of their future dramatic creations or to create paper backdrop scene panels to be pinned on the curtains at scene changes.

NATURE'S STAGE

Two main components are necessary for a stage: a platform and a frame. The frame may be made from rich red velvet curtains or a plain wooden rectangle, but whatever the material, its purpose is simply and clearly to provide a threshold between everyday life and the world of drama. For this project, I pulled the planks for the platform from a pile of scrap wood and found the branches in the woods. The "curtains" are made from surplus cloth napkins but could easily be made of any scrap fabric you have lying around.

- 2 boards, 6" × 24", at least ¾" thick
- 2 boards, 2"–4" × 11", from ½" to 2" thick
- 4 sturdy branches, fairly straight, about 2" in diameter (These will be the main vertical posts; their length depends on the height of the marquee you would like.)
- Screws of various lengths (about ½" longer than the wood you are trying to screw through)
- 1 medium-sized branch, around 1½" in diameter, longer than 24" (for the front marquee)
- 2 medium/small branches, around 1" in diameter, 12" or longer (for the side curtain rods)
- 1 medium/small branch, around 1" in diameter, 24" or longer (for the back curtain rod)
- Small finish nails
- Scrap fabric
- Ribbon

STEP ONE

Place the two 24" boards next to each other on a flat surface so they make a rectangle roughly 12" × 24". Place the 11" boards perpendicular across the first two boards, about 6" in from the ends. Secure with a couple of screws on each side.

STEP TWO

Cut two of the four sturdy (2" diameter) branches to a length of about 24". I chose to leave one end natural so the top of my theater would be a bit more organic looking, but you can trim both ends if you need to or you like the look better. Cut the other two pieces, in the same fashion, to a length of about 18".

STEP THREE

On the side of the platform with the supports, place a small mark roughly 1½" in from each side of each corner. Where lines drawn from each small mark intersect at a right angle, make another mark. (You will then have four corner marks for drilling.) Predrill a hole through the top of the platform at each of the four marked places and in the center of the bottom of each 2" post with an ⅛" drill bit. This makes screw-

ing the stage together much easier and lessens the possibility of splitting the branches. It also makes it simple enough that kids can put it together with a screwdriver after an adult has done the prep work. Once you have finished the predrilling, screw each post in place with the two longer posts in front.

Note: If you don't have a drill bit, you can screw the pieces together by driving a screw through one of the marks on the bottom of the platform until the point is just sticking out the top. Take the flat end of one of the longer 2" diameter branches and center it over the exposed screw. You should be able to push it down over the tip of the screw. Holding the branch securely, screw the rest of the screw in slowly. If you hear the branch begin to crack, back out the screw a bit and then go forward again.

STEP FOUR

Now that you have your platform and all of the vertical supports, it's time to attach the marquee in front and the curtain rods along the sides. Attach the branches to the supports by hammering in small finish nails or by screwing them together. In either case, due to the small diameter of each branch, I suggest predrilling the holes for the nails and/or screws first. As for placement, the height of the marquee and the rods is up to you. If you have prefinished fabric such as cloth napkins for the curtains, then I would place the three rods at a height that matches the width of your napkins. In my opinion, the marquee looks better when it is a bit higher than the rods, which also leaves room for a sign should you wish to make one.

STEP FIVE

With the stage complete, all you need now are curtains! For the stage shown here, I took a few old napkins and sewed on 12" pieces of ribbon folded in half (to make two ties) about every 3"–4" along the top edge; then I just tied them on. If you are working with unfinished fabric, you can either leave the edges raw or finish them by folding the fabric over and sewing it in place with a sewing machine or by hand.

12

Navigating the Imagination

The stars are bright above the boat. The waves slowly lap against the sides as the water gets incrementally shallower, until you hear the soft, heavy crunch of sand when you reach the shore. It's dark, but the moon is coming out from behind a low cloud bank, and the outlines of sloping hills and mountains begin to appear against the night sky. As you leave the boat, you make note of your surroundings on a scrap of paper, turn around, and walk forward.

At one point, maps were made by explorers without the aid of the GPS, satellites, and advanced mapping technologies we have today. We often see maps as pure scientific data, and why would we think otherwise? We can type an address into our car's navigational system and follow its directions to a destination, almost down to the foot. On a smartphone, we can see an aerial view of ourselves moving through the landscape, while we watch the hills and mountains pass by our windshield. In this modern era, we pretty much know exactly what's just around the bend. Yet that wasn't always the case.

For those early explorers, maps were made from personal observation. Each document was a reflection of a particular individual's perception of a space, how that person saw the world in his or her time. Because the explorers used what they had on hand, maps also came in all different shapes and sizes. There were cosmological maps, stick maps, and even three-dimensional, handheld maps (these early Inuit maps may be by far my favorite), each representing a particular vantage point at a specific time in history.

Childhood is a very important time in everyone's personal history. It's a time when you see the world in a way you'll never see it again. Size, shape, and distance are relative to interest, understanding, and perspective. We've all had the experience of returning to a favorite childhood spot and feeling it was almost foreign to our memory of it. It's not that the location has changed; it's that we've changed the way we see the world. Our perspective shifts physiologically, emotionally, and intellectually. But what if there were a way to find your way back to the space you inhabited as a child? What if you had a map of your childhood?

Mapping childhood may seem like an abstract concept, but it's no different than making any other sort of map. All you have to do is draw a picture of what you see. The distinction between real and imaginary worlds is less concrete for a child than it is for an adult. So a map of childhood will most likely reflect that soft line. Real locations can mix with imaginary kingdoms. Homes may be joined by castles and enchanted boats. However they come together, they'll be a perfect likeness of a particular time in a child's life. Every day is a new landscape. Those shifts in perspective happen hour to hour, minute to minute. Children can see the world through one lens in the morning and another in the afternoon. The topography of childhood is in a constant state of transformation. Maps can mark these changes. Maps are made to remember how to get back to important places, and *childhood deserves a good map.*

ADVENTURES IN CARTOGRAPHY:
MAKING YOUR OWN MAPS

From height measurements scribed directly on doorways to photos and scrap-books, we've always looked for ways to capture and recall those precious mo-ments of childhood. Yet many of these attempts mark only the physiological changes that happen as a child grows and changes from baby to toddler to kid to adult. Making and collecting the maps of childhood can be a way to capture just a bit of how children see the world through their own eyes. This section lists a few different ideas for various types of maps, but they are just a start-ing point. The maps you make will be inspired by the way your family sees the world from exactly where you are standing right at this moment.

If there is one thing that is definitely more predominant in childhood than at any other time, it's the world of fantasy. There are entire universes' worth of territory to explore and maps that don't exist (at least not as tangibly as they do in childhood) outside that time. Mapping those spaces in that moment can preserve them forever. How do you find your way to the kingdom of the elves from your back door? What do the enchanted mountains where the wizards live look like? Where do hobbits build their villages?

Taking the time to map these sorts of places not only crystallizes them in time, but it also expands your child's understanding of them, what they look like and feel like. To make accurate maps, cartographers need to know the area they are mapping like their own backyard. Like the stones on a path they travel every day. Children mapping the world of fantasy are no different. They have to dive into those spaces feetfirst with intention and intensity. They have to live in the neighborhoods of their imagination.

Even if your family doesn't move houses or apartments often, a map of where you live can change much more frequently than you might think. Owing to the fact that how we use and move through the spaces we inhabit shifts from month to month and year to year, a map of important features might change as often as daily. So making quick maps of favorite locations can be a great way to watch one space change over time.

I say "quick maps" because a fast map can more accurately depict preference and point of view than a map that is made over a long period of time. For example, when someone asks you about your favorite music, your first answer will most likely be what you are enjoying at that moment. When given a longer time to think about it, you might choose something else for different reasons. Since these maps are about how you see your world in a specific moment, there is a beauty in keeping them simple and fast.

Often we think of maps as two-dimensional sheets with colors and keys to help translate their lines to physical entities. But many maps are already three-dimensional. From topographical maps to Inuit carvings and papier-mâché globes, mapping can be a sculptural experience.

Inuit mapmaking techniques are perhaps some of my favorites. These tactile maps are hand carved from wood and have a sense of place that is both personal and experiential. To understand the landscape these maps depict, you have to hold one in your hands and run your fingers over the contours to reveal the craggy shorelines and sloping hills. They ask you to feel the world you're moving through.[1] Making three-dimensional maps at home can involve many materials, from soap to modeling clay to sticks and string.

MEMORY STONES

Collecting rocks has long been a way to collect memories of places and times. Stones from a particular location have a

way of transporting you back to the moment or place where you found them.

Growing up, my mother had a treasured box of rocks that her mother had collected as a child. They were housed in a wooden box with a hinged lid that my grandmother had painted and decorated when she was nine or ten. Opening it, I could almost see the places she wandered through, the trips she took, and what piqued her interest as a child. Memory stones serve essentially the same purpose, but they go a step further. By painting pictures or writing words on the stones, you can tell a story in many different ways.

HIDDEN TREASURES

Treasure maps, oh treasure maps! I think I made a million of them when I was a kid. Filled with sea monsters and rough waters, distant islands, shimmering jewels, and golden coins. Treasure maps are a wonderful outlet not only for creativity but also for dreams of adventures. What do those faraway lands look like? How would you get there? Who lives there? What kind of treasure is waiting to be found? Daring and exhilarating in all the best ways, a treasure map can be a beautiful snapshot of what a child imagines the world looks like just beyond the horizon.

MOMENT TO MOMENT

Mapping moments may seem like a difficult task, but like anything else, moments have a size and a shape, a weight and a presence. For a kid, birthdays, the arrival of new siblings, or simply a really great day at the park might be big moments. Abstract images like big and small circles drawn over a free-form calendar can be a wonderful way to remember how those important moments felt and when they happened—whether they were big events or small, day-to-day interactions.

STORING YOUR MAPS

Perhaps the most important part about making maps in childhood is storing and keeping them. Because, like all maps, they are made mostly for future reference, as a way to find something or someplace you haven't visited in a while.

Boxes or bags, folders or jars, file cabinets or drawers—a special place for keeping maps can take many forms. It need only perform a singular task: to preserve them for the cartographers so that, in years and years, they can come back and see all of those places again. They can find a way back to the lands of their childhood and, perhaps, share those lands with a child of their own.

PART THREE

Play

Potential energy: a lesson in the physics of childhood.
Play as compass and guide.

FORCE

It's a simple object, really. Not much bigger than a silver dollar. The edges are soft and round, partly from design and partly from use over the years. At first glance, it might be an old pocket watch, but inside the cover, there are no gears. No sprockets or complicated Swiss mechanisms—just a pin, an arrow, and a plain dial with four letters printed on it: *N, S, E,* and *W.* When everything looks the same, it's hard to tell in which direction you should go. You can try to follow the path of the sun. You can use your knowledge of flora and fauna to clue you in to your bearings. Or you can tap into that magical, invisible force that directs us all and use a compass.

We use a million different tools on a daily basis, and each has its own specific rank in our lives, depending on the service it provides. Some tools are good to have, but we can live without them. Some tools are more important, and some tools are necessary. A compass is exactly that: necessary. No matter the location, a compass has the map. From open desert to shady forests, it can lead you to the right path. But keeping you on track is not the asset that makes a compass indispensable. Rather, its ability to let you go off that trail is its real accomplishment. With a compass in hand, you have the freedom to get lost.

I love getting lost. Whether it's in the woods or a moment, nothing beats the feeling of being completely immersed in where you are. It's a hard thing to do these days, and it's always been a little difficult for me, which perhaps is why I appreciate it so much. There is an art to getting lost. To letting go of the idea that there's a right way to move through a space or a situation. To letting go of control and expectation, and allowing life to happen as it happens. The process of getting lost is a bit different for each person, but there is one rule that's always true: to enjoy getting lost, you have to know you can somehow find your way back. A compass will always bring you home.

Compasses come in all shapes and sizes. They can be gold and ornate, or they can be made of scuffed and dented green metal. They can be a simple needle in a glass of water, or they can be a feeling—an internal force urging you in a particular direction. We all know that sensation. The tidal pull that moves us forward, that guides our choices and our actions. Some call it intuition, some call it morals and ethics, some say it's spiritual; but whatever the term, the end result is the same. It gives us a sense of direction in the wilds of the world we wander, in the forest of our daily lives.

Children need that navigational force as much as the rest of us, if not a bit more. They need the ability to lose themselves in the world as they learn about it. They need to feel like they can move through its hills and valleys without fear or hesitation. Luckily, childhood has its own magnetic force, one that helps direct children in their actions, relationships, and education. A force that takes them wherever they want to go and always brings them home: *play*.

GRAVITY

For every experiment, there's a control: one singular element that is constant, against which everything else can be measured. Without a control, there is no way to find patterns, no way to see systems, no way to under-stand how the world works. Gravity is an amazing control element. It's always there, quietly pulling, keeping everything right where you left it. No matter how much you challenge its standing, like a bull, it holds its ground.

If play is the magnetic force that drives the compass of childhood, trust is its control. When children trust their environment, they feel safe. When they trust the constants of their surroundings, they can experiment. They can push the boundaries of their experience.

For the past few years, each fall, just as the hot days make way for cooler evenings, a one-ring circus pops up in a small park near my house. Over-night, a series of trailers roll in—some of them modern with all the amenities, some small and simple, tableaus of travelers from the past. The diversity of their styles matches the array of their inhabitants. Each is distinctly unique, yet somehow an integrated part of the same machine.

Their routine is a practiced one. Bleachers and supports take shape through actions that have been repeated a thousand times before. The only variant is the location where it happens. Everyone knows their job, and they do it well. In no time at all, the characteristic strings of twinkling lights signal the completion of construction. The tent is up, and soon the whole neighborhood will be able to see the show that happens inside. When I was young, the magic of the circus was just where you would expect it to be—in the sparkling costumes and high-wire acts, in the majestic horses and the red clown's nose. The circus made the world of fantasy come alive right there in front of my eyes . . . even if only for an hour of cotton candy–infused delight.

Visiting it again as an adult, I saw something different. I saw the balancing act that forms the foundation of each trick, each second in the spotlight. The way the clown would jump into the crowd to attract our attention while the equestrian performer dealt with a spooked horse. I saw the seamless mechanics of the crew as they supplied each act with the tools they needed, even before a hand reached out in full extension for the next prop. I saw the trapeze artist rely on the grip of her partner, leaping forward without a shred of hesitation. I saw the architecture of trust that allowed each moment to pass beyond the constraints of the real world and directly into the fantastic.

Trust comes in all shapes and sizes. It comes from parents, grandparents, caregivers, and friends. It comes from knowledge and education. But like gravity, its measure comes only from its effect on the objects around it. The true measure of trust only happens when you act in its orbit.

For kids, trust means freedom. It means they can live in the spotlight of that sawdust-covered ring. They can fly through the air, taking risks and making leaps, relying on the gravity of their world to do exactly what they've come to expect of it: to always be there.

POTENTIAL ENERGY

A few fibers twisted together to make a piece of string. Not exactly the most mysterious object in the world. We've all seen it a million times; in fact, I have hundreds of feet of it in my house at any given moment, rolled onto a ball, looped on a spool. In the present, string is just . . . string, but it's also so much more. It *can be* so much more. A ball of string is actually a mass of potential. Stretched between the ends of a curved piece of wood and pulled tight, it propels an object through the air. Knotted and extended over a river, it becomes a bridge. Tied around logs, it makes a raft. String can become almost anything with a little work, care, and energy behind it.

Every object in the world has energy, it has the ability to do work on another system.[1] Stones that lay there lifeless can become tools that shape, form, and even become houses. Wood can be crafted into baseball bats that send a ball soaring into the air. Energy is everywhere. But finding a way to harness it is a bit more complicated.

Most people in the twenty-first century think about the creation of energy on a fairly frequent basis. From fossil fuels to passive solar, wind, and water, we're on a constant search for new methods of gathering and storing energy. We do this because we need it for everything. We need it to power our lights, run our computers, heat our homes, and build our future.

Potential energy is stored energy. The law of the conservation of energy states that energy is "never lost and never gained."[2] When the string of a bow is pulled back, the energy used to do so doesn't just evaporate, it has to go somewhere. So for each inch you pull it back, the string fills with more energy, and its tension grows.[3] As long as you hold it there, it lives in the realm of potential, waiting to be released, to find its trajectory.

It takes a lot of energy, a lot of care, to bring a child into the world. From a physiological standpoint to an emotional one, parents, caregivers, and teachers pour energy into a child. And like the bowstring, all of that energy is stored, building and growing with each second until the moment it's released. An arrow moving though the world, feeling its own gravity, following its own compass.

THE PHYSICS OF CHILDHOOD

Force, gravity, energy, play, trust, care—all terms that exist in relation to the physical world, to the science of the everyday. All properties that work with and around each other. All part and parcel of the physics of childhood. They are the physical constants of a child's universe. Through the force or influence of play, children navigate the world. Through a knowledge of gravity and trust, they experiment inside it. Through energy and care, they make it their own.

Getting lost can take you to new places you wouldn't have necessarily found otherwise. Getting lost in play can take you to new worlds. When you let play be your guide, it can take you to an entirely new universe. . . .

13

Seeing Sound

As a kid, I was your standard orchestra geek, hauling my cello back-pack around, trying not to bump into doorways or knock unsuspecting classmates down in the halls as I made my way through them. I loved mak-ing music, no matter that I couldn't really play all that well. With a simple stroke of my bow, I could make sounds I couldn't have imagined before I picked it up. I could make noises that made people turn around. I could make music that made people move. My cello was its own sort of magic wand. I learned very early that sound is a powerful thing.

Yet like most powerful, magical things, the inner workings of sound are a bit mysterious. Sure, we can hear it easily enough, but we can't see it happen. We can't watch sound waves move through the air. We can't ob-serve their path from object to ear. For a child, this can make sound a rather abstract concept. Unless, that is, you can find a way to make sound visual.

Although we can't see sound, we can see the reactions it creates, and we can investigate the processes that make it happen. Nature is a great place to start looking—it's been using sound for as long as it's been around. Crea-tures of all shapes and sizes use calls and vocalizations to communicate in countless ways. The calls can be warnings, homing signals, or invitations for play. They can be loud, low, high, or soft. They can be a single sound or an entire orchestra. The natural world is full of millions of examples of sound as play, song, and signal.

One thing is astoundingly clear: whatever its end use, sound is a call to action. That fact is built into our DNA. We take full advantage of it the moment we pull in our first breath and let out an echoing cry. Sound is one of our first tools for exploring the world. It helps us understand space and distance; it helps us form connections between actions and activities (such as drumming and clapping); and it helps us identify animals, people, places, and things. But like any great tool, to get the most out of it, you have to understand how it works. You have to look under the hood and take a gander at the engine. And if there was ever an engine for sound, it's a musical instrument.

From bellowing bagpipes to rumbling drums and singing strings, musical instruments leave no stone unturned in exploring the world of sound. Sound may be invisible, but that doesn't mean it leaves no trace. Like building a picture from a puzzle, instruments (and the way they each produce frequencies) are the pieces that construct the image of sound. Understanding how a resonator box works, how two tiny reeds create the tone of a large wooden bassoon, and how a tensioned string changes its pitch will give you the key to the whole picture . . . to seeing sound.

PAINT CAN BANJO

One of the best things about sound is that it's everywhere, and you can make it with anything. Often we think of instruments as objects crafted only by a careful hand with years of experience. Not many of us would venture to make a violin or build a piano from scratch. Yet instruments are not limited to such highly precise constructions. In fact, they can be as simple as a few stones in a metal tin. For this basic banjo, an empty can, a stick, and three pieces of string will have you making music in no time.

- 1 pint-sized paint can
- 1 straight stick, about 2" in diameter, 18"–24" long
- Small nails
- 3 small wood screws, 1" in length
- Wood scraps (or a bag of bass wood scraps from a craft or hobby store) for the bridge and the nut
- 2 small bolts with matching nuts (small enough to fit in the lip of the paint can)
- 4 small washers
- 30-pound nylon fishing string, about 90" long
- 3 medium-size eye screws (with about a ¼" eye)

STEP ONE

Lay your open paint can down on its side. Place the end of the stick on top of the can near the opening, and rest it there. With a pencil or marker, lightly trace around the stick. Using a small nail and a hammer, poke three holes through the can inside and at least a ¼" from the edge of your traced circle.

STEP TWO

With a screwdriver or screw gun, attach the neck (the stick) of the banjo to the paint can from inside the can with three small screws through the holes you just made. This step can be a little awkward due to the size of the opening on the can, but with the holes already in the metal, the screws should glide through fairly easily. If you are setting this project up for children to construct on their own, you can also predrill the wood to make the process even more effortless.

STEP THREE

Once you have the neck attached to the body (the can), you can set up the nut and the bridge. The nut is the piece of wood that the strings will go over near the top of the neck, and the bridge is the piece of wood near the bottom of the banjo on the body. To attach the nut, simply place a piece of scrap wood (one that isn't too thick and measures a bit wider than the neck) near the top of the neck and secure it with a small nail. If you can get two nails in, even better.

For the bridge, I like using bass wood scraps, because there's often a number of different thicknesses of wood strips in a given scrap bag and they are easy to cut to size. (They're a little soft, but the strings aren't going to have that much tension anyhow, so it shouldn't be an issue.) You can also use whatever scraps you happen to have around. To attach the bridge, place the scrap wood toward the bottom of the can, just across the opening. With a hammer, drive a small nail through each side of the wood into the groove for the paint can lid. You may not make it all the way through, but you will at least leave an indent. If there is only an indent, take your bridge off and use a nail to complete the holes. If the hole is too small for your small bolts, simply widen it by driving a bigger nail through the hole. Attach the bridge to the paint can with the nuts, bolts, and washers.

STEP FOUR

To attach the strings, poke three holes in the groove for the paint can top below the bridge. Make sure the center hole is centered on the banjo and place the others roughly ½" to either side. (See photo on page 155.) Take three pieces of the nylon fishing string (each about 30" long) and tie a knot near one end of each piece. From inside the can, push the strings through the holes so the knots stop them from going all the way through. Pull the strings over the bridge to the top of the banjo. About 1"–1½" from the top of the neck, tie an eye screw onto each string and cut off the excess fishing line. Screw the eye screws into the top of the neck, winding the string as you go. Now all you have to do is tune your strings and start playing!

Note: If the strings are touching the neck or the body anywhere, you can remedy this by making the bridge and the nut a bit thicker. Either replace them with thicker pieces of wood or glue thin strips to the pieces you've already made.

STEEL DRUM

I've always loved the soft, melodic tones of a steel drum as well as its history of being made from found materials. In homage to this tradition, this drum is constructed from a one-gallon paint can and has a handy strap so you can take the music with you wherever you go!

- Felt scraps
- 2 dowels, ½" in diameter, 12" long
- Needle and thread and string
- Hot glue
- Colored string or yarn (optional)
- 1 gallon-sized paint can
- Earplugs (optional but recommended)
- Ribbon or cotton strap material
- 2 nuts and bolts
- 4 washers

STEP ONE

It is good to make the felt mallets first so you can use them to help you find your preferred tones while making the drum. To begin, cut your felt into two ¾" wide strips long enough to wrap around the dowels. Wrap a strip around the tip of each dowel and sew the side seams closed. Close the open top by running a few stitches back and forth. After you've finished sewing, pop off the felt tips and place a drop of hot

glue on the ends of the dowels; replace the felt. This makes sure the tips stay where they're supposed to. If you like, you can also wrap some colored string or yarn around the handles for decoration.

STEP TWO

Using a hammer (a ball-peen hammer is best since it has a rounded head, but any old hammer will work) and with your earplugs in, shape the bottom of the paint can by hammering from the center outward. The metal is fairly soft, and it works well when you start from the center of the indent and move in a circular motion outward. It will take several passes to see real progress (especially on the larger indentation), but it shouldn't take much longer than a few minutes. Once you have your center complete, repeat the process around the outer ring, making five to six small indents.

For the drum pictured, I made a large indentation in the center and then a circle of smaller ones on the outer ring. The depth and size of the indentations will affect the tone, so make sure to try out the drum with your felt mallets along the way.

STEP THREE

Using a power drill, drill a hole on the side of the can, close to the indented bottom and in line vertically with the handle on that side. Repeat on the other side. Measure the length of ribbon or strap you would like, add 12" to this length, and cut it. Poke a hole in your fabric strap 6" from the end on either side. Attach the strap to the can by placing the bolts (with washers) through the fabric and then the holes you just drilled; secure it in place with the washers and nuts on the inside of the can. Tie the excess strap around the metal handle at the point where it connects to the can (this should be directly below your bolts) on each side.

Note: Be careful after drilling the holes, as there can sometimes be sharp edges left on the inside of the can. I like to use a small file to knock these off and then sand the inside and outside of each hole with a little sandpaper.

SUGGESTED ACTIVITIES

• Start your instrument-making session by exploring how objects make noise. Bang on pots and pans. Put paper clips in a paper bag and shake them. Flex baking sheets to make thunder sounds.

Hold up a baking sheet, hit it with a wooden spoon, and then place your hand on it so you can feel the vibration.

- Play with sound in space. What does it sound like when you play music in a big room? How about a tiny closet filled with clothes? What does the same song sound like outside?
- Explore amplification by playing your banjo normally, then resting the bottom on a table with open space under it and playing. What happens?
- Make shakers by placing stones, beans, rice, seeds, and so on in metal tins and shaking them.
- Make a spoon clapper by tying two spoon handles on either side of a stick and hitting them with the palm of one hand, while holding the stick with the other.
- Write songs about your daily adventures.
- Draw pictures to go with your songs.
- Make "music videos" by animating these drawings either in a flip book or by scanning and editing them on your computer.

14

Stillness

Stillness is not a word we would necessarily associate with childhood. There is so much growth, movement, and energy that the quiet moments are often outnumbered. But it is for this exact reason that stillness is so important. It provides a space for processing and absorbing the activities of the day, for quieting the chatter of questions and thoughts that constantly circle in our minds, for being right where we are. Yet for most of us, particularly children, finding those moments of quiet can be difficult without something to focus on. While an adult may meditate, children play games.

Games of skill are the perfect conduit for moments of stillness in a child's day. First and foremost, they're games, which means they are—by default—fun. If you ask children to be quiet for five minutes, it's like asking them to be silent for a million years. Yet if you invite them to play a game that requires focus, they might be quiet for an hour without even noticing it. Games like archery, bocce ball, lawn bowling, and croquet all have the same process; they combine focus with calculated movement through space. Stillness paired with cause and effect.

If quiet gives us space to take in the world, understanding cause and effect shows us how to move through it. With games of skill, you have both. Each action has an effect. If you throw the ball too hard, it may miss its mark. Aim an arrow too much to the left, and it will fly past the target. Through the simple pursuit of precision, children gain an understanding not only of the world of physics but of the harbingers of lifelong success in any and every field: practice, patience, and perseverance. The best part of all is that these invaluable skills and abilities are gained while doing something equally important . . . having fun.

BOWS AND ARROWS

One of my favorite childhood pastimes at summer camp was archery. Camp for me was a beautiful chaos of friends and activities from the moment I woke to the second I fell asleep midsentence while talking to my bunkmate. I was never without something to say or listen to, and in retrospect, I think that is exactly why I loved my afternoons spent with bows and arrows. It was a quiet time of skill, concentration, and—something my nine-year-old self would never have thought of—finding my center. It was years (actually decades) before I picked up an archery set again, but from the moment I pulled back the first arrow and let it go, I felt it. That quiet space with one simple goal to contemplate, where everything else falls away.

Now you might be thinking, "Kids and arrows? Not for me!" But this simple set I whipped up from a few things around the house is safe (see the notes that follow), fun, and a great way to make room for a little quiet contemplation in your child's day. You might use the time constructing the bows and arrows to talk about the different cultures that have used them historically, as well as to learn about the physics involved in shooting an arrow.

MATERIALS

- 3–6 regular wine corks and 2 sparkling wine corks (If you don't have any of these in your home, craft stores often sell wine cork assortment packs.)
- At least 4 bamboo garden stakes, standard 5' length (more if you'd like to make a lot of arrows)
- Tape (I like gaffer's tape due to its cloth surface, but duct tape would work as well.)
- Medium-weight cotton string (often available at your local hardware store)
- 1 yard canvas or cotton duck in white or natural
- Ribbon (optional)
- Fabric paints (at least three different colors)
- Beeswax or jojoba oil (for waterproofing the canvas)
- Natural water-based paints (biodegradable would be best)

STEP ONE

Drill a hole down the center of each of the sparkling wine corks, from top to bottom, to form the handle (the big bulb at the top makes the perfect spot to rest your arrow as you aim, and the bulb at the bottom makes for a comfortable handle). Slide them down to the middle of a bamboo stake with the bottom ends together, and tape them together in the middle of the stake. It's good to drill the holes just slightly smaller than the bamboo so the corks will stay where you put them.

STEP TWO

Tie the string at the top of the stake about 4"–6" down from the end (I wrapped it around a few times, knotted it, and secured it with a little tape). Bow the bamboo and decide where you want to attach the other end of the string. Once you have that distance,

measure out the length of string you need, plus about 6" extra. At the loose end, tie a taut line hitch knot (see the image on page 164). To make sure the line won't slip up the stake, make a stop for it by wrapping a good amount of string around the stake at the point where you want to hook your line and secure that with tape as well. Hook the loop around the stake and pull the knot up the line to your desired level of tautness.

STEP THREE

For the arrows, drill holes in the center of three to six regular wine corks to about half the depth of the cork (again, the holes should be slightly smaller than the stakes). The length of the arrows will contribute to the distance they will shoot (short ones will travel less distance than longer ones on a string of the same tension), so some experimentation at this point is good. The arrows pictured are about

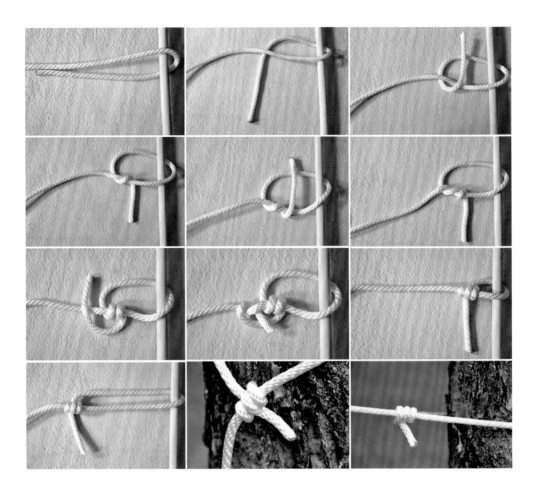

18" long. Play around with lengths and line tension until you find the right length for you. Once you know how long you would like your arrows to be, cut three to six pieces of bamboo to that length.

Make the groove at the back of the arrow, where it rests on the string, using a small metal file. If you don't have one, you can use the same handsaw you used to cut the arrow lengths; just be sure to clamp the bamboo to something and to keep both hands on the saw, as it can slip before it gets a good hold. The saw method should be completed by adult helpers.

To make the washable cloth target, cut the fabric to your desired target size, about 28" wide or so. You can either leave the edges raw or turn them under and finish them with a sewing machine. You can also sew two ribbons to each corner to function as ties for hanging the target, or you can sew ribbon loops onto each corner for the same purpose.

With a pencil, draw out the shape of your target. For this project, I made my target a star, but you can do a traditional circle, a heart, a square, and so on. Once you have the outline of the shape you want, draw the smaller versions of it inside the main shape (these will be your "target rings"). Paint the different sections with different colors of fabric paint. Once your target is completely dry, rub it with soft beeswax or jojoba oil to make it water-resistant.

Play! Dip your cork arrow tips in washable paint and test your skills. Rinse off the target with a hose or in the sink after each use.

Adjusting the tension in the string as well as the length of the arrows allows you to determine the arrows' velocity (that is, how far and fast they go). Shorter arrows don't let you pull the string back very far, making them more gentle since they don't have as much tension behind them. The same is true of leaving a little more slack in the line.

With these two options, you can customize your archery set to be age appropriate for your family. Also consider drawing a line on the sidewalk or laying a rope out on the grass to delineate the arrow range so kids won't venture into it. And as always, make sure there's an adult to help out.

A variation on traditional lawn bowling, in this game, you can either roll the striped stick at the pins or toss it toward them. These two options, in conjunction with color-coded pins, allow for many different games using the same seven sticks.

- 7 small sticks or logs, 2"–3" in diameter, cut to 6"–7" long
- Paint
- Jojoba oil or beeswax

MAKING THE GAME

Take six of the seven sticks or logs (leaving the straightest and roundest aside) and paint one end of each with a color; these are the pins. I chose to make two pins of each color, but you can paint them each a different color or paint half of them and leave half natural. For the last pin, paint each end the same color and then paint at least one stripe around the middle to indicate it as the tossing pin. Once the pins are painted, you can seal them with jojoba oil or a natural beeswax to protect the paint.

To play, arrange the pins so they are standing together in a group. Walk a short distance away and determine your throwing line. From there, toss or roll the tossing pin to knock down as many pins as you can. See below for more suggestions.

ACTIVITY SUGGESTIONS

When using the log pins, you can simply play a traditional bowling game in which each pin is worth a point, or you might assign different point values to each color. These points could be obtained either by rolling or tossing the striped stick. Additionally, you might make the game a bit more difficult and try to knock down only one color, with each person or team having a specific color (like bowling and billiards combined). If you enjoy the smaller set, make more pins to make the game more complex.

On the River

With the sun just barely changing the sky from black to the purple and pink of early dawn, I was out of bed. It was quiet and cool, and almost everyone else was asleep. More people than you would think could fit in a tiny log cabin that was over one hundred years old, but I was small and my footsteps were light, so they all kept right on dreaming. As I approached the front door, I could see him sitting there.

He was larger than life, my grandfather. Not just in character (although this was true as well) but also in size. He was a big man, around six feet four. Wearing his cabin uniform of an old denim shirt, a pair of jeans, and some well-worn cowboy boots, he folded himself into a rickety metal lawn chair outside the front door. You would never have guessed by the look of him that he had grown up on the cobblestone streets of New York City. Although he had, I think his heart was born in Montana. Stepping outside, I moved to join him. He was going over the tackle box, making sure everything was in its place. Setting up his fishing pole and mine. I was still in my nightgown, and he put the fishing vest on me. I remember the weight and smell of it. A little musty, like old army tents, and heavy from the line weights in the pockets. I loved that vest. You didn't get a special vest like that unless you were about to do something really important. After I found my boots and managed to pull on some jeans under my PJs, we made our way to the river.

As we walked through the grass, the rest of the world slowly changed from open vistas to dew-covered greenery. I was small, and the grass was very high in most places, so it felt like a jungle as I pushed my way through, grasshoppers landing on my head and shoulders when I disturbed their rest. I could tell we were getting close to the water when the air grew heavy and cool. Although it was well into the summer months, the water was still fast and high in some places from the snowmelt. To get to the quiet spots, we had to wade through the fast current. With every step, I could feel both of my feet lift off the ground for a moment, my only tether the tight grip of my grandfather's hand. I knew he would never let me go. Because of that, I wasn't afraid. I loved the high water because I could feel safe and free at the same time. I could feel the full power of the river but not get lost in it.

After our trek, we finally made it to the sandy bank on the other side, right next to a deep, calm pool where there were often fish. My grandpa set down the tackle box and unhooked the lure on my pole while deciding which fly he would tie to his. Once everything was settled, he pointed me in the direction he thought I should cast and then walked down the shore a bit, all without a word. We spoke very little while we fished.

For hours we stood on the bank and cast, watching the sun start to make its way over the hill. Some days, birds would land in the trees near us or deer would wander down to get a drink. Once an owl rushed right over our heads, but for the most part, the only sound was the river and the slow click of our reels as we pulled our lines in. On this particular day, there were no special sightings or big catches. To tell you the truth, I don't remember taking anything home at all, but I was never much concerned with the spoils of our fishing trips. I just liked going down to the river with my grandpa. There, standing on the shore, I felt connected to the world, like I could feel every single part of it in my bones, in the air in my lungs, in the blood in my veins. I was seven years old.

—*Sarah*

15

The Long Road

The purpose of a machine is to automate a process and make that process as efficient as possible. The Industrial Revolution bears great witness to this. Through manufacturing, we can make a thousand shovels in an hour with the same workforce it would probably have taken to make twenty. Machines are masterful tools. But what happens when you take the efficiency out of a mechanized process? What happens when you make a complicated machine to perform a simple action? Absurd results, you might say, but there is a lot more than that going on.

In some instances, the best route to a new destination isn't the shortest distance. Sometimes it's the process of getting there that holds the best lessons. Life is a good example of this. Even so, not many of our pursuits echo this hypothesis, which is exactly why we need people like Rube Goldberg.

Rube Goldberg was a sculptor, engineer, inventor, and cartoonist famous for his cartoons of absurdly complex machines that performed simple, mundane activities. He was so noted, in fact, that the term "Rube Goldberg" appears in the dictionary as an adjective to describe something that is "fantastically complicated" and improvised in nature.[1] An activity as succinct as using a napkin might involve the construction of a machine that would require a string, a spoon, a parrot, and a rocket, along with a number of other components. Yet for all their kitsch and humor, the machines Goldberg drew performed an invaluable service. They put a spotlight on the beauty of taking the long road.

Childhood is a long and wonderful road. It's full of fantasy and idiosyncrasy. Everything is larger than life to a child, and the ideas generated during childhood often reflect that sentiment: they are big, ostentatious, and beautiful, even if nonsensical. In an adult world, children's ideas may sometimes seem inefficient, but to a kid, they are the components of a perfect machine.

You learn a lot of things by taking a simple process and complicating it. You learn how and where disparate systems intersect. You learn about cause and effect. You learn the principles of the physical sciences. You can even learn about chemistry (if you use, for instance, a baking soda–and–vinegar reaction to start a ball rolling down a board). But most important, you learn how to think a complicated process through from beginning to end. You learn how to be an inventor.

Inventors see the world through a lens of potential. Each element has a value and a relationship to an idea. There is no such thing as an inconsequential detail. Because of this, inventors see the world that exists, as well as the world as it could be . . . they see the world through a child's eyes.

RUBE GOLDBERG MACHINE

The process of building a Rube Goldberg machine is about exactly that—process. Although the end result is definitely part of the destination, every curve in the road along the way is just as important. Each component of the machine is a chapter in a novel. It has its own peaks and valleys, its own drama and subtlety, its own opportunity to tell a story. How that story unfolds is completely up to you. The following are some guidelines to get you started.

To build a machine, you have to know what function you would like it to perform. Since a Rube Goldberg is about extrapolating simple actions, a great way to get into the mind-set of this type of engineering is to build a machine that selects the purpose for your Rube Goldberg machine: to make a Rube Goldberg for a Rube Goldberg. Since this type of engineering is often idiosyncratic, chance operations (processes that produce random results) can be a good

way to go. Here are a few suggestions for different types of selection machines, but by all means, feel free to make up your own:

- Cut different shapes into the top of a cardboard box and find objects that match those shapes. With a marker, write different machine functions on each of the various objects. Put them inside the box and tape it shut. Turn the box so that the holes face the floor and shake it until one of the

shapes comes out. Make a machine based on the function that is written on it.

- Write one function on each page of a blank notebook. Place the book in front of a fan and make a machine based on the first function you can read.
- Write different functions on small pieces of paper and tape these pieces to dominoes. Line up the dominoes in your favorite configuration. Bounce a rubber ball on the ground in the direction of the dominoes until it hits one of them, starting a chain reaction. Make a machine based on the first domino that fell.

Different types of machine functions may include but are definitely not limited to the following:

- Pouring a glass of water
- Waving a fan
- Opening a curtain
- Flipping a light switch
- Feeding a cat
- Knocking down a house of cards
- Pretty much anything you can dream up

Like anything, some materials are more advantageous for building a Rube Goldberg than others, but don't let that stop you from trying out whatever you happen to have on hand. Raid your cupboards, your recycling bin, and your junk drawers for anything and everything that looks like it might be useful. Here are some of my favorite materials to use.

Rope

It's no surprise that rope is at the top of the list. From working pulleys to swinging sticks and raising buckets, it's hard to picture a Rube Goldberg that doesn't use rope in one way or another.

Pulleys

Raising and lowering objects is one of the best ways to set off a chain of events, and pulleys make this happen smoothly each and every time. From lifting a board so a ball rolls off the other end to dropping a rock that pulls on a string and dumps a bucket of water, pulleys can keep a machine on track.

Cloth

Cloth is great for catching objects that fall, holding objects that need to be raised (like a pile of rocks), and much more. Not to mention it's great for making flags and embellishments.

Rocks

Rocks are nature's weights. They can be used to hold something down or knock something over. Balance and gravity play a big role in building a Rube Goldberg, and each of them have quite a bit to do with weight.

Pinwheels

I love pinwheels as embellishments in a Rube Goldberg, but sturdier versions can also be part of a delivery system for dropping a marble or a ball onto an angled board and so on.

Dominoes

Dominoes are pretty wonderful, because they can travel across a distance (by knocking each other down), and they can also function as weights (when the last domino to be knocked down falls off a platform, changing the balance of the machine).

Small Buckets or Pails

Buckets full of water can be poured out to start another interaction. A bucket full of rocks can act as a counterweight for a pulley. A tilted bucket with a hole in the bottom can catch a marble and send it off in a new direction.

Sticks

From pinwheels to shelves to levers, sticks can be used as the base structure for many different functions on a Rube Goldberg machine. They can swing from a tree and knock down a rock, they can make a bridge for marbles to roll down—really, the possibilities are endless.

Marbles

With a little momentum behind them, marbles can go a long way toward starting or continuing an interaction. They can roll down boards and spirals; they can function as weights when they roll off one platform to land on another; and they can easily make their way across long distances when used in large machines.

Lids

Lids to canisters of various sizes can be used for many different functions.

They can be attached to a wooden stick to become a platform; they can be used as paddles to push objects forward; and they can work as stops when attached to a string.

This cursory list is just a starting point. The best Rube Goldbergs are the ones that take advantage of whatever happens to be lying around. With an eye for potential, you can transform anything into a beautiful machine.

PHYSICS

It's no surprise that a machine based on a chain reaction involves a lot of physics. But don't let that word frighten you off. Everything we do, from waking up in the morning to opening a door or riding a bike involves a lot of physics. Learning the principles of physics by building a Rube Goldberg is one of the most natural processes there is. Through play and trial and error, important terms and concepts become the

everyday vernacular of problem solving. When children can see and feel the forces they are dealing with, they can grasp those concepts easily. Here are some of the more important physical concepts involved in building a Rube Goldberg.

Potential Energy

Potential energy, or the energy of position, is energy stored in an object or a system due to position. For example, when a bow is not drawn, it has no potential energy; it is in its equilibrium position and is happy to be there. When you pull the string of the bow back, it has energy due to the position in which you are holding the string. As soon as you let go of the string, it releases that energy and returns to its original position.

Rube Goldberg machines are all about potential energy. Objects held in a position away from where they usually like to be are the perfect candidates to start and continue a chain reaction. A rock held up by a string (giving it potential energy) will swing down and knock over a bucket when that string is untied. If that bucket is holding a board at an angle, then the board will fall down and knock over a chain of dominoes, and so

on. Most of the time spent building and designing these types of machines revolves around figuring out how to create and release potential energy.

Gravity

Every physical interaction on the planet has a relationship to gravity. It is a constant force that acts on everything from leaves to bouncing balls. Gravity is what makes things fall to the ground; it's what gives them weight. The force of gravity slows down objects that are moving up and speeds up objects that are falling down. Understanding the effect gravity has on objects and interactions will help you design your machine.

Balance and Equilibrium

If there is one thing that's constant across all Rube Goldberg machines, it's the use of balance. Like a house of cards, a Rube Goldberg often functions on groupings of objects that rely on a thin margin of balance to remain stable. The slightest change in condition and they can come crashing down. A rock precariously balanced on a ledge will easily fall when tapped with a swinging stick. A marble will roll down a ramp when pushed over the edge by a rolling can.

Speed, Velocity, and Friction

Objects gain and lose speed depending on the forces or elements with which they interact. Objects moving downward will gain speed the farther they fall, and the opposite is true for objects moving upward. Friction also plays a big role in speed. A ball rolling down a gravel slope will roll much more slowly than a ball rolling down a smooth board.

Basic Mechanics and Simple Machines

Simple machines like wheels and axles, pulleys, levers, and inclined planes all play a big part in designing a Rube Goldberg. Understanding how they work will help you to build infinitely more complex interactions. What's the best way to learn about simple machines? Experiment! Play with pulleys and weights, adding different weights and using multiple pulleys at the same time. Learn about levers by balancing a board on a rock. Try putting weights (pennies or buttons) on either side when the rock is in the middle, then move the rock farther to one side. How many pennies or buttons do you need to put on each side to balance it this time? Roll a ball down a slightly inclined board, then try it again with a bigger incline. What happens? Try as many variations as you can think of.

16

Exploration through Play

The world is full of clocks. We have them on our wrists, phones, and computers, in our cars and houses. The ever-advancing tick of time is never beneath our notice. It's how we measure our days, the length of our seasons, the years of our lives. Yet childhood, in its purest state, is timeless. Days, weeks, years, seconds, minutes, and hours are all interchangeable, defined only by the excitement or interest surrounding a particular activity. As adults, we have a tendency to try to put a clock on childhood. Some of this is necessary; otherwise, children wouldn't often show up to school on time or go to bed at an hour that provides them with the rest they require. For the most part, children listen to our clocks and play by our rules. We shuttle them from place to place and urge them toward activities we believe will provide them with the tools they need. In all fairness, we should listen to their clocks as well: let them lead and find a path for the day. Let them take us through their world to new territories.

When I was a kid, my mom drove us all to school each day following the exact same route. Like clockwork, we'd scramble down the stairs and into the car with precisely nine minutes to spare before the morning bell. Once she turned the key in the ignition, I could close my eyes and tell you exactly where we were at any given second. I knew each bump in the road, the timing of every traffic light, the sounds of each neighborhood we passed. The space between school and home was one I knew well and could illustrate without hesitation. That is, until the day I was old enough to walk home from school with my brother. From then on, it was an entirely different experience. My whole life, I'd been following an outline, a perimeter, and now I could see everything that was inside—a world I never even knew existed. Leaving the path, wandering over new terrain, can do that for you.

Whether it's your route to school or work or just your daily routine, repetition can leave everything outside of that routine's orbit in the dark. Finding a way to break that repetitive process can turn on the lights. In 1958, Guy Debord wrote an essay on just that subject, on the *dérive*.[1] A *dérive* is an open-ended journey through a space (cities, parks, houses, and so on) where the elements in that location "guide" you along an unplotted path to an unknown destination, an experience unfettered by schedules and expectations. Debord believed that spaces of every kind have an influence on our mood and behavior. By opening our senses and sensitivities, we can allow those influences to guide us. In breaking our routine, we can see a new world right inside the one we look at day in and day out. For adults, this is often a conscious act, but for kids, a *dérive* is their primary method of navigation. It's how they see the world. They engage with the architecture of their environment and follow their intuition to new spaces. They live authentically in every moment. They live through play.

Play and exploration go hand in hand. They are two parts of the same organism, each working to broaden the horizons of the people engaged with them. Play is not just an activity; it's also a map and a guide. It can show you an entirely new world and provide a way to navigate the one you already know. "Playful wandering" is just another term for exploration.

Standing at the shore of childhood is like standing at the shore of the ocean. Its vastness is incalculable. Its waves beat in an ever-changing rhythm, their waters filled with hidden life and immense beauty. Play is the ship that navigates these seas, limited only by the time we take to sail it. So step on board, and leave your watch at home.

EXPLORATION BAG

Letting go of schedules and expectations can be difficult at times, especially when most of our lives are built around these restrictions. But unstructured play and exploration work best in an open environment with as few limitations as possible. In the real world, this often isn't an option on a daily basis, so when the moment arrives, it's great to be ready.

A number of times in the past, some wonderful opportunity came along, and due to my lack of readiness (knowing where in the world my tent was or how I would ever be able to gather all the materials I needed for a three-day trip in one hour), I couldn't go or felt hesitant about making the commitment. Since then, I've remedied the situation with a simple ready-to-go box that is filled with a tent, sleeping bags, camp cookware, camp stove, dishes, silverware, soap, rain gear, bug spray, headlamps, binoculars . . . pretty much anything I think I may want on an impromptu trip to the woods. Now when the planets align and open the window to a few days of pure exploration, I can grab that box and be out the door in no time. It's no different for a kid; although a big box of supplies isn't necessary for a day of exploring, a good bag of tools sure doesn't hurt. Although any old bag that you have on hand will work, sometimes making a special one just for exploring can be a great way to get excited about future expeditions. Here is one option for a quick envelope bag, but it can easily be transformed into a drawstring bag if you prefer not to sew the flap. It can also be a messenger bag if you'd prefer not to make adjustable straps.

MATERIALS

- Exploration Bag pattern (see page 214)
- 1 piece fabric, 13" × 31" (I like canvas for this, but it can be any sturdy fabric you have.)
- Needle and thread or sewing machine.
- 2 pieces ribbon, ¾"–1¼" wide, 6" long each (to hold the key rings/D-rings for the straps)
- 4 metal key rings (or D-rings, if you have them)
- 2 pieces ribbon, ¾"–1¼" wide, 24" long each (for the straps)
- 1 piece ribbon, ¾"–1¼" wide, 2" long (for the closure loop)
- 1 piece ribbon, ¼" wide, 12" long (for the ribbon closure)

STEP ONE

On one short side of the 13" × 31" piece of fabric, fold the edge over by ¾" and sew it in place to finish the edge. On the other short side, find the center and measure out 3" to either side; make a small mark in these spots. This will be the bag top. Measure 6" down from the top corner on each side and make a mark. With a ruler and a pencil, draw lines between the marks at the top and the ones on each side of the fabric to create the shape for the envelope flap (see the figure on page 214). Cut the cloth about ¾" above each line to account for the seam allowance.

Fold over the top edge by ¾", making sure it is folded in the same direction as the bottom edge, and sew it in place. Fold over each angled side by ¾" and sew the edges in place. Fold the bottom edge of the bag up to the bottom of the angled top edges. Make sure the right sides of the bag are together and the seams are facing out. Sew along both sides ½" from the edge. Turn the bag right side out.

STEP TWO

With the bag body complete, it's time to add the adjustable straps. Take the two 6" pieces of ribbon and fold each end under twice by ¼"; sew the ends in place. Slide two metal key rings or D-rings onto each ribbon and fold the ribbons in half. Pin each ribbon in place about 1½"–2" from the top of the bag and the same distance in from each side, with the ends facing the bottom of the bag. Sew over each ribbon three to four times to secure.

Take the two 24" sections of ribbon and fold one end of each ribbon under twice by ¼"; sew the ends in place. With the finished ends toward the bottom of the bag, pin each ribbon in place about 1½"–2" from the bottom of the bag and the same distance in from each side. Sew over each ribbon three to four times to secure.

Weave the ends of the straps through the key rings. Test out the length of the straps on your little explorer and then trim the excess and finish the ends so they won't fray.

STEP THREE

To make a ribbon closure for your bag, take the 2" section of ribbon and finish each of the cut edges by folding the ends under and sewing them in place. Position this piece horizontally on the front of the bag, centered between the sides and just below the flap. Sew the ribbon in place along the left short edge and the right short edge, leaving the center open to act as a loop.

Fold the 12" piece of thin ribbon in half, and sew the folded section to the underside of the flap in the center, about ¾" from the edge, with the two ends hanging below the flap. This will allow you to tie the bag closed through the loop you just finished.

EXPLORATION TOOLS

Now that you've found or made your bag, it's time to fill it with everything your little explorers might want. Since it's their bag, I think it's great to have them make a list while suggesting a few items like these:

- A shade fort (a piece of cloth with long string or thin rope sewn to each corner) for reading and drawing
- Blank cards (4" × 6") for making nature cards
- Small cloth specimen bags for collecting treasures
- A notebook
- Something to write or draw with
- A compass
- A magnifying glass
- Binoculars

The most important thing is that kids feel like they have everything they might need for a big expedition. Once all the items are assembled, place them in the bag and have your little explorer try it on to see if it's too heavy. If it is, take a few things out; it's never fun to go on a long walk with a bag that's too full.

SUGGESTED ACTIVITIES

Once you're out the door, anything is possible! Here are a few options:

- Play follow the leader and take turns being the guide to new locations; maybe even play a game at each new destination.

- Look for a specific color and let that guide you from point to point.
- Follow different birds in the trees for as long as you can.
- Take your favorite numbers and pair them with compass directions (north, south, east, and west) to create directions (like fifteen steps north, ten steps west) to follow and see where you end up.
- Draw pictures of your favorite birds; make up games with those pictures.
- Draw your favorite plants.
- Read books to flowers and trees.
- Write stories about animals and new adventures.
- Identify cloud types and look for shapes in them.

Trees

As a kid, I always liked trees, no matter what the season was. Growing up in Connecticut, we were blessed with majestic hardwood forests interspersed with seventy-foot pines and blue spruces. The winters would render them dark and ominous, whirring and moaning in the strong winds of our ever-present nor'easters. Winter would finally yield to spring, making way for the maples and oaks to create great canopies above the old winding roads. I remember the katydids and crickets signaling summer and lasting just long enough to appreciate the September cooling. This triggered the explosion of color from the maples and mighty oaks that began raining down leaves in massive quantities; my dad and I would corral these leaves into piles that my sister and I would dive into over and over.

Around age eight, I mastered the art of the jungle gym and could walk fearlessly on top of the monkey bars. This was a harbinger of things to come, and soon I began to look at the giant trees as fair game for an aspiring climber. I was under five feet tall, so this was a challenge. But armed with a stout rope and with visions of Mount Everest, I began my quest for higher places. I started by tying some big knots in the rope and swinging it fast so it would encircle a lower limb. Then I figured out how to walk up the trunk, which was no easy feat for a skinny little guy.

Within a week or two, I had completed my ascension to the fifteen-

or twenty-foot level of a large pine, and cast a determined gaze upward. I can still feel the breezes change and smell the bark, the sap, and the needles as I moved higher, checking my footing and handholds, managing my fear as best I could. I remember the sensation of things getting smaller and the tree beginning to sway, which caused me to pause and gather courage to finish the journey. I began to feel the tree's trunk and branches getting smaller and the skies getting bigger as I broke through the canopy. What an amazing revelation! What a view! My senses exploded, as did my heart in my chest. I just held on with a vicelike grip and began to take in this extraordinary space that I had never seen before. The clouds in late spring were a thick cumulous mass full of shadows, angels, faces, and spaces. I imagined flying like Superman through this new landscape.

I could have stayed up there all day and dreamed and designed many new adventures if it were not for a persistent sound that broke my concentration. "Jooooeeeyyy! It's time for lunch. Where are you?" My mother was calling me, grounding my great aspirations with thoughts of my next favorite thing—food. I replied in my best sweet voice, "Up here!" I started waving, and she saw where I was and gasped, "Are you OK?"

"Yes!" I said cheerfully, "I'll be right down."

I made my descent to where I could see my mom below, shaking her head and smiling. When I landed in front of her she patted me on the head and said with that concerned and practiced look that all moms have perfected, "Let me know next time, when you're climbing the tall trees."

I turned and looked back up at where I had been. It was really a fantastic place to be, way up there. It filled my soul with a sense of wonder and adventure that I will always treasure. That experience has served me well through life, and I am reminded daily to practice that discipline of wonder and imagination with my family and in business. In a true metaphor, the high road is always the good road, so cherish the view!

—Jonas

17

No Instructions Required

Sometimes I go to the grocery store with a detailed list in hand. I have a specific plan for what I am going to make, and I have plotted out exactly what I need to prepare it: a quarter pound of fennel, six ounces of arugula, three ounces of parmesan cheese, and two baby artichokes. No more, no less. Some days I look in the fridge and think, "Potatoes, leftover green beans, and eggs. . . . What can I make with that?" I often find that the dishes I make from the random scraps in my cupboards are much more rewarding than those I plan. For starters, whether the unplanned dishes are stellar or just OK, I always feel like I've pulled off a magic trick. I had "nothing," and I made something edible, even enjoyable, out of it. With a planned meal and a carefully followed recipe, I end up expecting a particular result and then judge my efforts based on that expectation. With the impromptu meals, I don't have any expectations. Childhood games can have a similar process.

There are a million games out there—board games, outdoor games, card games—all with a set of specific components and a list of rules to follow. Sometimes this is exactly what you need. But sometimes you need to make your own rules. As a kid, I never much liked games with too many guidelines (as evidenced by my culinary proclivities). I would inevitably forget one thing or another from the long list and end up losing a turn or the game as a result. Yet I loved to play games with other children, particularly those that just "happened" in the schoolyard, the backyard, or the living room. Those games were always so fresh and new.

For a child, there are a lot of rules to remember in a given day. Stop and look both ways before crossing the street. Don't talk to your deskmate during class. Don't bounce basketballs in the kitchen. Don't eat sweets before dinner. Each of these guidelines is there for a good reason, but as a sum, all the everyday dos and don'ts can leave children without much room to make their own choices, to have agency in their actions. Creating a time when the rule is "no rules" not only makes a space for children to follow their intuition unabashedly, but it also makes the follow-the-rules parts of the day much easier to accept.

Impromptu play is play at its best: pure, straight from the source, free, and beautiful. It allows children to work out who they are and what they would like to become in their own perfect little microcosm. It helps them learn to navigate social and group dynamics and to hone their skills in everything from basic problem solving to math and physics. But like all good things, impromptu play needs the right ingredients and the right environment in which to grow and flourish. Luckily, those components are easy to find. Just add time, attention, and a willingness to play the game . . . then watch your garden grow.

GAME SEEDS

Whereas too many rules can sometimes dampen creativity, keeping a wide variety of tools and materials on hand can spur it on. Inspiration comes from many places, so even the most unlikely materials can often turn into an amazing game, like beautiful plants emerging from tiny, bumpy seeds. This section gives you a list of a few "game seeds" that I love to keep within arm's reach, but it's just a start. Your seed drawer can keep growing and growing.

STRING AND ROPE

I can't say enough about the power of rope and string. I talked about it earlier in reference to potential, so it's no surprise that rope and string are at the top of my list for important game materials. Whether it forms a spiral ground target for beanbags, is the connecting line between tin cans for playing telephone, or provides the main element in a good old-fashioned game of tug-of-war, a rope can be all you need for hours and hours of fun. It's a finish line in a race; the guarded perimeter around a flag; the connection between a tree branch and swinging, high-flying freedom.

FLAGS AND BANNERS

Flags, flags, oh beautiful flags. Perhaps because of their cultural and historical importance, perhaps just because they are beautiful objects, I have always loved flags. From medieval to modern, a few bits of fabric sewn together can instantaneously transform into an amazing and important object. The same transformation happens in games that incorporate them. Whether it's capture the flag, a scavenger hunt, or a relay race, flags provide a tangible goal to reach for. Using handmade flags that kids design

with their own colors and images? Even better.

JUMPING SACKS

Who doesn't love a good jumping sack, right? No matter your mood, put your feet in a jumping sack, and you're guaranteed to be laughing in three seconds flat. Whether they're made from old pillowcases or sewn from fabric scraps with sturdy handles, jumping sacks can shake things up just enough to start hours of playful antics and games. Is it raining outside? Paint designs and/ or team crests on your jumping sacks so they will be ready to go as soon as the sun comes out. While you're at it, why not plot a jumping sack obstacle course?

BEANBAGS

Bags filled with beans (or rice or barley or whatever you have on hand) are infinitely versatile. They're great for juggling, for playing oversized tic-tac-toe beanbag toss, or for throwing adventure bags (on a hike, each player attempts to toss his or her bag and get it to land on different goals along the way, from rocks and stumps to low-hanging tree branches; the more difficult the toss, the higher the points). Want to make them even more versatile? Sew a different color on each side, and give them different values.

TIN CANS

A collection of clean, opened tin cans has a lot of game potential. There are the classics like kick the can and telephone, but cans may also be made into a pyramid for "can bowling" or used as minidrums or relay batons.

BUTTONS

A bag of old buttons is great to have in the mix as well. They are wonderful game pieces, checkers, and tokens—not to mention, amazing scavenger hunt finds.

CARDS

Everyone knows the versatility of a deck of playing cards. There are millions of different games you can play with them, so they are an obvious choice for a game seed. But going along with the concept that fewer rules equal more open-ended creativity, I also love a blank deck of cards. Just keep a stack of card-sized paper in a bag with a writing implement. That way you can create cards with any theme or numbering system. You can even design blank cards into a game that can be changed or altered to become anything a player desires when he or she receives one during a game.

BALLS

Ball games are as old as time, which makes them quite a game seed. There are, of course, the standards like soccer, baseball, softball, basketball, football, and kickball to consider. Then there are the playground games like four square, dodgeball (with soft foam balls), and handball. Needless to say, a few balls of different sizes and shapes open the door to a lot of classic games, as well as the creation of new ones.

NOTEBOOKS

You may be thinking, "Notebooks? Really?" Yes, notebooks. Perhaps one of the most important game seeds is a simple, blank notebook. When you're making up games on the fly or planning out an obstacle course, having a place to keep all of that precious information is priceless. The best thing about notebooks? They turn into amazing game books that document years of playful experimentation and fun.

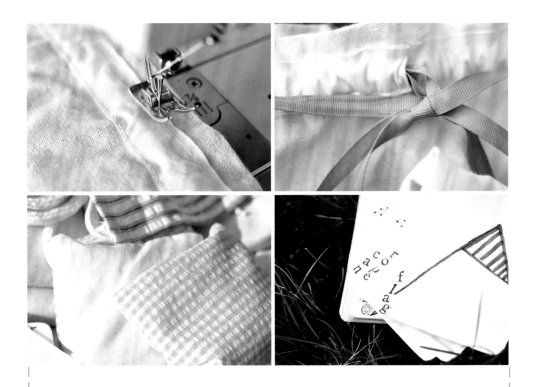

SIMPLE DRAWSTRING GAME BAG

It's one thing to have all these materials available; it's quite another to know where you left them last. Having a game bag to store them in means they're always ready when you are. Best of all, you don't have to decide what you're going to play with before you leave, since you can keep everything in one easy-to-find spot. The bag itself can even become its own random game generator. Simply make a deck of cards that includes a card for each object in the bag, choose three cards, and make up a game with the corresponding objects.

- 1 old pillowcase or scrap fabric
- Needle and thread or sewing machine
- Medium-weight string or ribbon, about 1 yard
- Fabric paint or stamps (optional)

FROM A PILLOWCASE

On the outside of an old pillowcase, near the side seam where the hem is, cut a small hole (about ½" wide) just through the top layer of fabric on either side of the side seam. Push the fabric in and under along the opening and secure it in place with a needle and thread, taking care not to sew into the bottom layer of fabric. Attach a safety pin to the end of the string or ribbon; push it into the first hole, through the pocket made by the hem, and out the other hole. Pull the draw-string through and knot it together at the ends. Voilà! You have a drawstring bag. Decorate it with fabric paints or stamps, if desired.

FROM SCRATCH

If you would like to make a bag from scratch, simply decide on the bag size you want and cut a piece of fabric that is the exact width and double the length. Fold it in half lengthwise with the right sides together, and sew up the sides. While the bag is still inside out, roll down the top edge by ¼" and crease. Roll it down once more, this time by 1", and sew it in place near the bottom edge.

Flip the bag right side out and insert the drawstring using the method de-scribed for the pillowcase option. If you would like a bit more decoration, you can sew a ribbon around the top of the bag to use as the drawstring casing. Measure out the amount of ribbon you need to encircle the top of the bag and add two inches. Cut this length and finish the ends by folding them under and sewing them down. Starting at one end, sew the top and bottom edges of the ribbon to the bag at the position you'd like to have the drawstring, leaving an opening at the front where you can insert the string.

18

Time and Space

Play happens in many ways. We usually think of it as an active process, but some of the most important play happens quietly, in our thoughts. As much as children explore the physical world through play, they navigate the world of the mind through the play of their imagination. Yet, as it is for many of us, finding a quiet place to sit and think can be harder than it seems. For the most part, we all organize our days around schedules and activities, things to do, people and places to see. Between work, school, extracurricular activities, and homework, it can sometimes feel like there isn't much time for anything else.

When I first began the process of writing this book, I sat down and tried to make a list of the "crystallized" moments of my childhood—those times that shaped my understanding of the world. I looked for the activities and events that marked my transformation from baby to child to adult. But I quickly realized that the majority of those moments happened outside of action and activity. Outside of the big "events" of my early years. Most often, the subtle shifts happened during lazy afternoons lying on the grass or in the hours I spent staring out the window at the shifting leaves of the tree in our front yard. In my attempt to make a list of activities, I had covered my page with two simple words repeated in every variation possible: *time* and *space*.

Time and space are two incredibly difficult things to pin down. They're big, abstract, complicated entities that orbit our lives and our thoughts, intrinsic to each moment yet completely intangible. Time is unstoppable. Its forward pace is the metronome of the days, weeks, years, and decades we experience. No matter how much we try to collect it, save it, and measure it, time slips through our fingers before we can get a good hold. Space is equally difficult to grasp. Even with all our maps and precise measurements of geographical locations, staring out into the ocean, I still could never tell you exactly how much I can see. Time and space are immeasurable, without context and comparison. Childhood is just the same.

Without the time and space to add context to a day's activities and compare actions to outcomes, experiments to results, life is just a jumble of data. The information is all there, but the key is missing. Yet with a little distance and perspective, everything can begin to make sense.

WISHING KITE

Flying a kite is essentially the definition of play: open, intuitive, and without a specific purpose outside of enjoyment. In a word, it's free. You can sit on a hill and let the wind take your kite high into the air until it's a small speck of yellow in an ocean of blue sky. You can be in the sky and on the ground all at once. You can be the line between the two. You can just be. Kites are built for distance and perspective. They are constructed around the concept of stepping back and looking at the whole picture. They can give you the tools to make your own key to the world around you. In addition to the distance and perspective that kite flying affords, it provides the space for something equally important: wishing and dreaming. It provides a place where thoughts can wander and accumulate, where they can run into each other in ways they wouldn't normally. This project combines those two activities. After building a sturdy cloth kite, kids can decorate detachable kite tails with their thoughts, wishes, and dreams. Then they can send them up in the air and out into the world. This kite takes a little time to put together, but since it is cloth, it can be washed and used over and over, whereas a paper one might be good for only one or two high-flying adventures.

MATERIALS

- Kite pattern (see page 215)
- 1 yard natural cotton muslin, at least 36" wide
- Needle and thread or sewing machine
- 1 yard ribbon, 2" wide (or 1" wide), in the color of your choice
- 1 yard ribbon, 1" wide, in the color of your choice
- 2 thin bamboo garden stakes or wooden dowels, $3/16$"–¼" in diameter, at least 36" long
- A spool of strong cotton or nylon string
- 36" × 2" kite tails in various fabrics and colors (make as many as you'd like to have on hand)
- Fabric paint
- Permanent markers

STEP ONE

Follow the measurements in the diagram to cut out your diamond kite shape from the natural muslin fabric. With a ruler, make a mark ½" in from the edge on either side of each corner. With a straight edge and a pencil, connect those dots so you have a ½" border on all sides. Trim the excess above where the lines intersect at each point.

STEP TWO

Fold the edges under twice by ¼". Crease the folds with a ruler or an iron and sew them in place. The corners might not match up perfectly, but don't worry about this; they will be covered by the corner reinforcements in the next step.

Lay the 2" (or 1" if that is what you have) ribbon across one of the corners with one finished edge of the ribbon aligned with the tip of the kite corner. Cut the ribbon so that it extends ½" past the corner at its widest point. Fold the ribbon under itself so that it mirrors the shape of the kite corner and sew it in place, sewing back and forth along the outside edge where the kite and the ribbon meet to make a strong connection. Trim any excess ribbon that sticks out

of the bottom of the pocket. Repeat this process for the rest of the corners.

STEP FOUR

Now it's time to make the tabs for the bowline. The bowline is a line of string that pulls at the edges of the horizontal wooden dowel to bow the kite outward. This helps the kite to fly well.

To make these tabs, take two 3" sections of the 1" ribbon, fold each in half, and sew the ends together securely. Flip the loop tabs inside out so the seam is on the inside. Place the tabs on the back of the kite on each of the side corners, on the opposite side of the fabric from the reinforced corner pockets. Position them so the folded edge of each loop extends past the apex of each corner by about ¼". Sew them down securely by hand, making sure not to sew the pocket on the other side closed.

STEP FIVE

Now you need something to attach the tails to. Make two more loop tabs, as described in the previous step, and place them near the bottom corner of the kite; sew them down securely.

STEP SIX

With all of the sewing complete, it's time to cut your dowels or bamboo poles. I like to do this now, because things have a tendency to shift during sewing. Place one end of the pole or dowel you're using for the horizontal crosspiece in one of its respective corner pockets; stretch the kite and mark where the tip of the other side lands on the wood. Cut the pole at that point. Do the same thing for the vertical piece.

STEP SEVEN

Place the horizontal pole in the kite first, followed by the vertical pole on top. Tie the pieces together with a little string where they intersect. For added support, add a ribbon tie near each corner. With the structure in place, mark a point under the poles near each corner. Remove the structure and center a 6"–8" piece of 1" ribbon over each mark, perpendicular to the line of the respective dowels. Sew each ribbon in place, then put the structure back in place and tie the ribbons around each pole at the corners.

STEP EIGHT

To make the bow in the kite, tie one end of a piece of string to one of the tabs extending from the corners at the ends of the horizontal piece. Stretch the string over the horizontal pole to the other side, tying it off at the other loop using an adjustable taut line hitch knot (see the figure on page 164). The bow you create should leave about 3" of space between the kite and the string.

Poke a small hole through each of the corner pockets at the ends of the vertical pole. For the bridle, tie the end of a piece of string to the pole at the top of the kite, then push it through the hole in the fabric to the other side (the face of the kite); extend the string down to the bottom of the kite, push it through the hole, and tie it off around the pole, being sure to leave some slack in the line (about 4" worth). If you'd like to reinforce these openings, you can sew around them with a few stitches.

Tie your flying string to the bridle about a third of the way down from the top, and all that's left is to design your tails.

STEP NINE

It's time to spend some time making wishes and drifting on daydreams. Draw, paint, and write the thoughts you'd like to send up in the air on the pieces of cloth you cut for your kite tails. These thoughts may be shared or secret, simple or complex; it's between you and the sky to decide.

Once you're finished making them, tie the tails to the kite through the loops at the base. To make the tails longer, simply tie more pieces on, end to end. Not only will they look great, but they'll also help the kite fly well.

SAVING WISHES

With all that time spent making wishes, they need a good place to rest once they've completed their flight. If they are secret wishes, they might need a bag to hide in. If they're shared wishes and dreams, they might be sewed into a banner or quilt, or they might simply be hung together on a hook on the wall, making a beautiful mass of color and intention.

MORE FUN WITH KITES

- Paint and decorate the kite too!
- Make sky stories by writing short adventures along the tail ribbons.

Then and Now

"When I was a kid, . . ." It's a phrase we all use on a regular basis. I've used it myself over and over in this book. It's a useful statement that helps differentiate the past from the present, one that illustrates a story in time. It's a true statement, but it's also completely false in one very important respect: childhood isn't something that can be put in the past tense.

We all grow up; there is no argument there. Physiologically, we can never go backward; we can't shrink in size or reverse our development. We can't travel back to the physical moment when we were three or eight or eleven, but that's not what I'm talking about anyway. What we're discussing is neither temporal nor physiological; it's not a calendar date or a distant memory. It's a perspective, a method of interpretation—childhood as a focusing lens on the present world.

In the perspective of childhood, potential is limitless, curiosity is an electrical current, and every moment is open to the possibility of the unexpected. Day-to-day life is filled with adventure and excitement. Roadblocks are just invitations to try a new route. The world is vast and expansive. In the perspective of childhood, everyone is a kid. We might not all look the same—some may be bigger than others; some may have brown hair and others gray—but we can all see through the same eyes . . . as long as we keep them open.

Templates and Patterns

The patterns in this section are shown at fifty percent. To use, photocopy them at 200 percent or download and print actual size patterns from www .roostbooks.com/imaginechildhood. Please use the patterns from this book for your own personal use.

SEASONAL CAPE
Enlarge by 200%

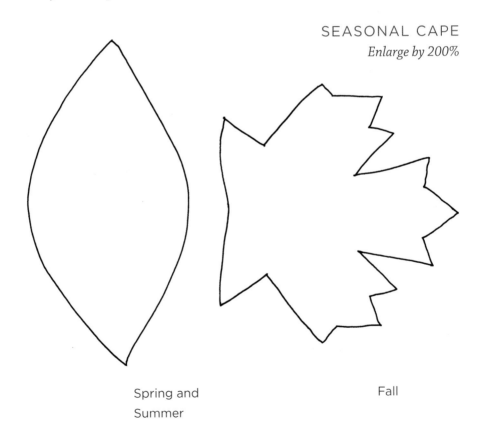

Spring and
Summer

Fall

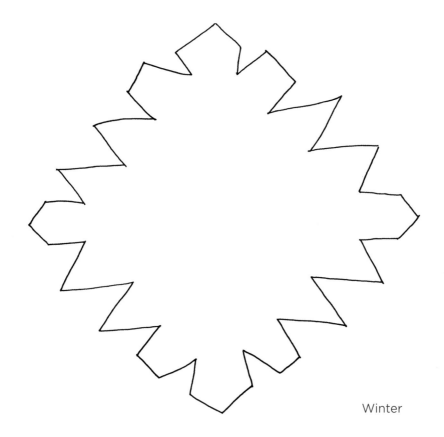

Winter

MAPLE LEAF HOUSE
Enlarge by 200%

BIRD OF PARADISE MASK
Enlarge by 200%

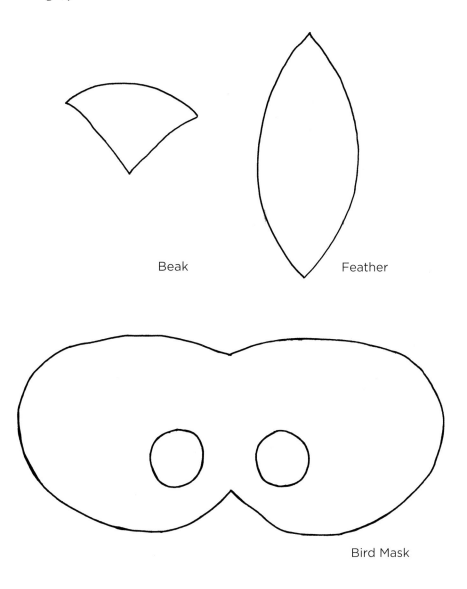

Beak

Feather

Bird Mask

MAGIC LANTERN
Enlarge by 200%

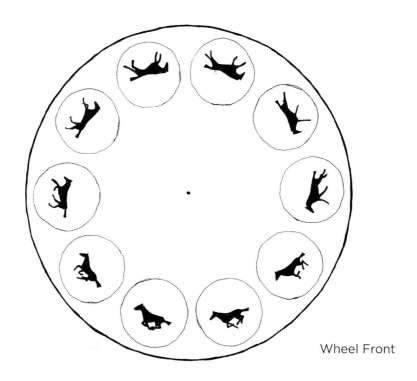

Wheel Front

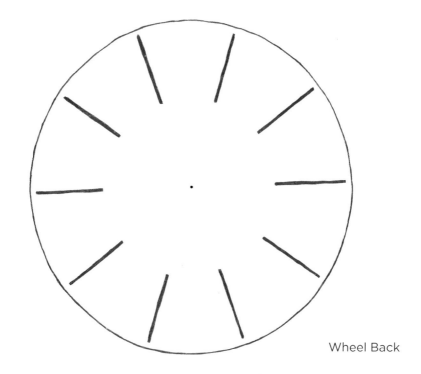

Wheel Back

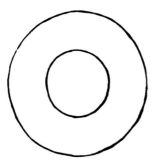

Viewer Frame

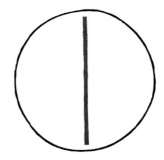

Shutter Top

EXPLORATION BAG

Use as a measurement guide

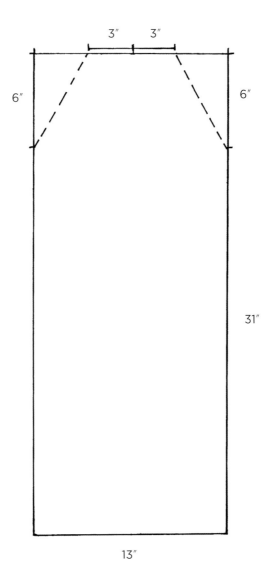

KITE

Use as a measurement guide

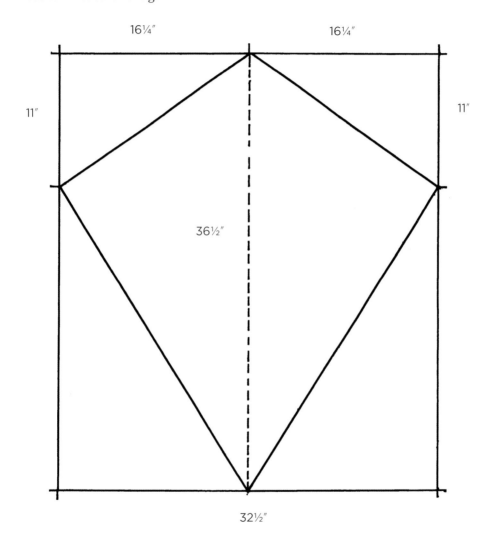

16¼″   16¼″

11″   11″

36½″

32½″

Notes

PART ONE: NATURE

1. Dick Proenneke, *Alone in the Wilderness,* directed by Bob Swerer (Fort Collins, Colo.: Bob Swerer Productions, 2003), DVD.
2. Joseph Bharat Cornell, *Sharing Nature with Children: The Classic Parents' and Teachers' Nature Awareness Guidebook* (Nevada City, Calif.: Crystal Clarity, 1979), 28.
3. Charles E. Beveridge, Paul Rocheleau, and David Larkin, *Frederick Law Olmsted: Designing the American Landscape* (New York: Rizzoli, 1995), 35.

PART TWO: IMAGINATION

1. Umberto Eco, *Semiotics and the Philosophy of Language* (Bloomington, Ind.: University Press, 1984), 28.

CHAPTER 10: BY THE SEA

1. George Buehler, *Buehler's Backyard Boatbuilding* (Camden, Me.: International Marine, 1990), 14.

CHAPTER 12: NAVIGATING THE IMAGINATION

1. *Maps: Finding Our Place in the World,* exhibition at the Field Museum of Natural History, Chicago, 2007.

PART THREE: PLAY

1. Walter Lewin with Warren Goldstein, *For the Love of Physics: From the End of the Rainbow to the Edge of Time—A Journey through the Wonders of Physics* (New York: Free Press, 2011), 171.
2. Ibid., 169.
3. Ibid., 171.

CHAPTER 15: THE LONG ROAD

1. Peter C. Marzio, *Rube Goldberg: His Life and Work* (New York: Harper & Row, 1973), 181.

CHAPTER 16: EXPLORATION THROUGH PLAY

1. Guy Debord, "Théorie de la Dérive," *Internationale Situationniste,* no. 2 (December 1958), www.larevuedesressources.org/spip.php?article38.

Resources

Many of the books and materials referenced in this book can also be found at imaginechildhood.com.

NATURE BOOKS

Cassino, Mark, Jon Nelson, and Nora Aoyagi. *The Story of Snow: The Science of Winter's Wonder.* San Francisco: Chronicle Books, 2009.

Cornell, Joseph Bharat. *Sharing Nature with Children: The Classic Parents' and Teachers' Nature Awareness Guidebook.* Nevada City, Calif.: DAWN Publications, 1998.

Driscoll, Michael, and Meredith Hamilton. *A Child's Introduction to the Night Sky: The Story of the Stars, Planets, and Constellations, and How You Can Find Them in the Sky.* New York: Black Dog & Leventhal Publishers, 2004.

Driscoll, Michael, Dennis M. Driscoll, and Meredith Hamilton. *A Child's Introduction to the Environment: The Air, Earth, and Sea Around Us—Plus Experiments, Projects, and Activities You Can Do to Help Our Planet!* New York: Black Dog & Leventhal Publishers, 2008.

Elpel, Thomas J. *Botany in a Day: The Patterns Method of Plant Identification.* Pony, Mont.: HOPS Press, 2006.

Herriot, James, Ruth Brown, and Peter Barrett. *James Herriot's Treasury for Children.* New York: St. Martin's Press, 1992.

Kirkland, Jane, Rob Kirkland, Dorothy Burke, and Melanie Palaisa. *Take a Backyard Bird Walk.* Lionville, Pa.: Stillwater Publishing, 2008.

Kroodsma, Donald E. *The Backyard Birdsong Guide: Eastern and Central North America. A Guide to Listening.* San Francisco: Chronicle Books, 2008.

Landry, Sarah. *Peterson First Guide to Urban Wildlife.* Boston: Houghton Mifflin, 1994.

Leslie, Clare Walker, and Charles Edmund Roth. *Keeping a Nature Journal: Discover a Whole New Way of Seeing the World Around You.* North Adams, Mass.: Storey Publishing, 2003.

Louv, Richard. *Last Child in the Woods: Saving Our Children from Nature-deficit Disorder.* Chapel Hill, N.C.: Algonquin Books of Chapel Hill, 2008.

Lovejoy, Sharon. *Sunflower Houses: Inspiration from the Garden—A Book for Children and Their Grown-Ups.* New York: Workman Publishing, 2001.

North, Sterling, and John Schoenherr. *Rascal.* New York: Puffin Books, 2004.

Peterson, Roger Tory, and Margaret McKenny. *A Field Guide to Wildflowers: Northeastern and North-Central North America.* Boston: Houghton Mifflin, 1998.

Pretor-Pinney, Gavin. *The Cloud Collector's Handbook.* San Francisco: Chronicle Books, 2011.

Rezendes, Paul. *Tracking & the Art of Seeing: How to Read Animal Tracks and Sign.* New York: HarperCollins, 1999.

Stokes, Donald W., and Lillian Q. Stokes. *Stokes Beginner's Guide to Birds.* Boston: Little, Brown, 1996.

Thoreau, Henry David. *Walden,* ed. J. Lyndon Shanley. Princeton, N.J.: Princeton University Press, 1971.

Young, Jon, Ellen Haas, and Evan McGown. *Coyote's Guide to Connecting with Nature.* Shelton, Wash.: OWLink Media, 2010.

NATURE WEBSITES

American Hiking Society. www.americanhiking.org.

Center for Biological Diversity. www.biologicaldiversity.org/index.html.

Children & Nature Network. www.childrenandnature.org.

The Cloud Appreciation Society. http://cloudappreciationsociety.org.

Convention on Biological Diversity. "Celebrate the Green Wave!" http://greenwave.cbd.int/en/home.

Cornell Lab of Ornithology, Cornell University. "All About Birds." www.allaboutbirds.org/Page.aspx?pid=1189.

Kideos—Videos for Kids. "National Geographic Videos." www.kideos.com/national-geographic.

NatureFind. www.naturefind.com.

National Park Service, U.S. Department of the Interior. www.nps.gov/index.htm.

National Park Service, U.S. Department of the Interior. "Explore Natural Sounds." www.nature.nps.gov/naturalsounds/gallery.

National Wildlife Federation. "What Is a Green Hour?" www.nwf.org/Get-Outside/Be-Out-There/Why-Be-Out-There/What-is-a-Green-Hour.aspx.

Oakland Museum of California. "Listening to Nature." http://museumca.org/naturalsounds.

USA National Phenology Network. "Nature's Notebook: Observe Plants and Animals." www.usanpn.org/?q=how-observe.

Wilderness Awareness School. www.wildernessawareness.org/index.html.

IMAGINATION BOOKS

Akerman, James R., and Robert W. Karrow, eds. *Maps: Finding Our Place in the World.* Chicago: University of Chicago Press, 2007.

Andersen, Hans Christian. *Hans Christian Andersen's Fairy Tales.* Selected and illustrated by Lisbeth Zwerger. New York: Minedition, 2006.

Bachelard, Gaston. *The Poetics of Space.* New York: Orion Press, 1964.

Beskow, Elsa Maartman. *Children of the Forest.* Stockholm: BonniorCarlsen, 2007.

Buehler, George. *Buehler's Backyard Boatbuilding.* Camden, Me.: International Marine, 1990.

Burgess, Thornton W. *Old Mother West Wind.* Illustrated by Harrison Cady. Boston: Little, Brown, 1960.

Burnett, Frances Hodgson. *The Secret Garden.* Adapted by James Howe; illustrated by Thomas B. Allen. New York: Random House, 1987.

Gombrich, E. H. *The Story of Art.* London: Phaidon Press, 2006.

Konigsburg, E. L. *From the Mixed-up Files of Mrs. Basil E. Frankweiler.* London: Walker, 2003.

Koopmans, Loek. *Any Room for Me?* Edinburgh: Floris Books, 2000.

Müller, Brunhild. *Painting with Children.* Edinburgh: Floris Books, 2002.

Perec, Georges. *Species of Spaces and Other Pieces: Essays.* Translated by John Sturrock. London: Penguin Books, 1998.

Saint-Exupéry, Antoine De, and Richard Howard. *The Little Prince.* San Diego: Harcourt, 2000.

Sendak, Maurice. *In the Night Kitchen.* New York: HarperCollins, 1996.

Smith, Keri. *This Is Not a Book.* New York: Perigree Trade, 2009.

———. *Wreck This Journal.* New York: Perigee Trade, 2007.

Weschler, Lawrence. *Seeing Is Forgetting the Name of the Thing One Sees: a Life of Contemporary Artist Robert Irwin.* Berkeley: University of California Press, 1982.

Wolfe, Maynard Frank. *Rube Goldberg: Inventions.* New York: Simon & Schuster, 2011.

PLAY BOOKS

Chudacoff, Howard P. *Children at Play: An American History.* New York: New York University Press, 2007.

Davis, Todd, Juli Stewart, and Nik Schulz. *Handy Dad: 25 Awesome Projects for Dads and Kids.* San Francisco: Chronicle Books, 2010.

Elkind, David. *The Power of Play: Learning What Comes Naturally.* New York: Da Capo Press, 2007.

Katzen, Mollie, and Ann L. Henderson. *Pretend Soup and Other Real Recipes: A Cookbook for Preschoolers and Up.* New York: Tricycle Press, 1994.

Martin, Laura C. *Nature's Art Box: From T-Shirts to Twig Baskets, 65 Cool Projects for Crafty Kids.* Drawings by David Cain. North Adams, Mass.: Storey Publishing, 2003.

Nelson, Peter, and Judy Nelson, with David Larkin. *The Treehouse Book.* New York: Universe, 2000.

Pawson, Des. *Handbook of Knots*. New York: DK, 2004.

Pelham, David. *Kites*. Woodstock, N.Y.: Overlook Press, 2000.

Smith, Keri. *How to Be an Explorer of the World: Portable Life Museum*. London: Particular, 2011.

Soule, Amanda Blake. *The Creative Family: How to Encourage Imagination and Nurture Family Connections*. Boston: Trumpeter Books, 2008.

Stiles, David R. *How to Build Treehouses, Huts & Forts*. Guilford, Conn.: Lyons Press, 2003.

Ward, Jennifer. *I Love Dirt!: 52 Activities to Help You and Your Kids Discover the Wonders of Nature*. Boston: Trumpeter, 2008.

———. *It's a Jungle Out There!: 52 Nature Adventures for City Kids*. Illustrated by Susie Ghahremani. Boston: Trumpeter, 2011.

Wiseman, John. *SAS Survival Handbook: The Ultimate Guide to Surviving Anywhere*. New York: Collins, 2009.

Yankielun, Norbert E. *How to Build an Igloo: And Other Snow Shelters*. New York: W.W. Norton, 2007.

PLAY WEBSITES

IPA World (International Play Association). http://ipaworld.org.

Natural Learning Initiative. www.naturalearning.org.

About the Contributors

Deb Olmsted currently lives and works on Bryn Du Farm in Colorado. Along with caring for the animals, she produces handmade Flower Fairies and Fairy Houses using wool from her herd of Jacob sheep. Among the many pursuits that preceded her cofounding of imaginechildhood.com, Deb raised four children and established Follow Your Heart, a Euro classic toy store in Denver that received many local and national accolades, including multiple features in *Country Living Magazine*.

Jonas Olmsted, a child of the fifties and sixties, spent most of his youth running around in the forests and fields near his home, undoubtedly contributing to his lifelong love of landscape architecture. A thirty-year veteran of marketing, business development, and capital formation, Jonas has worn many hats, but his favorites include designer, singer/songwriter, and dad. He currently lives in Colorado and works on business development at imaginechildhood.com.

Noah Olmsted holds a bachelor of environmental design degree from the University of Colorado and a master of architecture from Columbia University. After graduating from Columbia in 2005, he moved to Los Angeles, where he worked in the design and film industries. Noah is currently focusing on art and filmmaking.

Jared Olmsted lives and works in New York City. After receiving bachelor of arts and environmental design degrees from the University of Colorado, he went on to receive a master of architecture from Columbia University in 2006. He is currently a practicing architect, musician, and artist.

Jordan Olmsted currently lives and works in Boulder, Colorado. After receiving a bachelor of arts degree in art history and bachelor of science in journalism, she went to work for Imagine Childhood as a jack-of-all-trades, specializing in blogs and photography. In addition to her Imagine Childhood contributions, Jordan is a lifelong horse enthusiast and aspiring artist.

About the Author

Trevor Gainer

SARAH OLMSTED grew up in Colorado and spent much of her time exploring art, science, and the nearby foothills and mountains. After receiving a bachelor of fine arts degree from the San Francisco Art Institute, she spent some time as a freelance children's furniture designer/fabricator, which eventually led her to the Field Museum of Natural History. There she worked in exhibit design, developing interactive educational activities for permanent and traveling exhibitions before moving on to cofound imagine-childhood.com in 2008.